G14-95

Wool'n Magic

Other Search Press books by Jan Messent

Have You any Wool?

Needle Crafts series

Stitchery

Embroidery Design

Craft Library series

Knitted Gnomes and Fairies

Knit an Enchanted Castle

Knit the Christmas Story

Wool'n Magic

JAN MESSENT

SEARCH PRESS

First published in Great Britain 1989
Search Press Limited
Wellwood, North Farm Road,
Tunbridge Wells, Kent TN2 3DR

Copyright © 1989 Search Press Limited

Edited by Pam Dawson
Designed by Julie Wood
Assistant Editor Rosalind Dace

Photography by: Search Press Studios on the front and back
cover and on pages 3, 12, 20–22, 27, 35, 42, 43, 45, 46, 50, 51,
63 (below), 79, 80, 84, 88, 89, 93, 94, 97, 110, 111, 113, 122, 123,
131, 137; Jan Messent on pages 9, 13, 26 (below), 39, 62
(below), 63, 64–68, 70–73, 75–78, 81, 86, 91, 94, 95, 99, 101,
103, 105, 108, 119, 121; Binns Oddy Photography, Leeds, on
page 37; Keith Pattison on pages 38, 129; James Walters on
page 134. All black and white photography by Jan Messent.

The publishers and author acknowledge with thanks the
following, who have given permission for their photographs
to be reproduced in this book: The Bradford Industrial
Museum for *The knitted Merino – Harry Ram* on pages 9, 13;
Sterling Gallery for *What became of the perm?* on page 13, *Aran
sheep* on page 15 and *Shetland sheep* on page 26; the Knitting
Craft Group for *The four seasons* panel on pages 29, 40, 41, the
knitted patchwork panels on pages 30, 33, *Stalactite cave* on
pages 47, 55, the knitted sample on page 52, *Volcano hanging*
on page 57, the samples on pages 59, 61, the ring samples on
pages 82, 83, 85 and the canvaswork sample on page 93; Jean
Jobbings for *Sunset* on pages 91, 101; Jean Taylor for the
Seashore panel on page 105.

ISBN 0 85532 614 X

Typeset by Scribe Design, 123 Watling Street,
Gillingham, Kent
Printed in Spain by Artes Graphicas Elkar, S. Coop.
Autonomia, 71 - 48012-Bilbao - Spain.

Contents

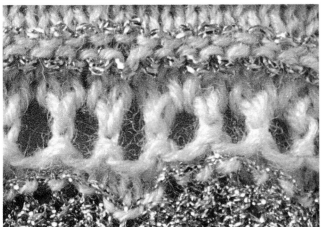

Introduction

As many textile crafts are related in terms of materials, structure and concept, it seemed sensible to me to assume that a book which combined some of these crafts would be likely to appeal to a good many people who are proficient at more than one. Embroiderers usually also know how to knit and crochet and, indeed, often use these two techniques as a means of creating texture in their work, just like using another piece of fabric.

Many knitters and crocheters also combine embroidery as a means of embellishing the background fabric. Though other books have touched on this combination briefly in passing, including my own books on embroidery design, none, so far as I know, have dealt with the tremendous possibilities in any depth. There is still much more to be said and many more ideas to be explored and developed, but I have attempted to draw attention to some of the livelier aspects of using yarns. Preference has been given in this book to those aspects which demand some thought and planning on the part of the reader, rather than an ability to follow pages of detailed instructions.

In short, this book is for brave spirits and genuinely creative people; there are few patterns or detailed instructions for the models and panels, mostly descriptions, diagrams and guidelines. This is in keeping with the best embroidery books, where readers are expected to glean ideas and then do some thinking on their own behalf. I hope that the ideas shown here will be seen as a challenge, as a springboard for the imagination and skills, with just enough information included to give the reader a good idea of what is involved, providing she/he has a reasonable, but not expert, knowledge of the techniques. The projects are not difficult, but they *do* require some decision-making on the part of the reader, so if you need detailed instructions on how to knit a rectangle to make a bag, the ideas in this book will not appeal to you.

Garments are discussed only as far as the 'ideas for design' stage; after that, you can use your skill and imagination to create your own original design. Nearly every other book on knitting and crochet will tell you how to go about making a garment fit; few books will tell you how to make it different and unique! This book aims to fill that gap; all *you* need is vision and courage. The time element is hardly worth mentioning; enjoyment is the main by-product, the unique garment comes a close second, the time taken to make it is quite irrelevant. If you have still not snapped this book shut and firmly jammed it back on to the shelf by this time, you're obviously adventurous enough to take the ram by the horns! So start gathering your yarns and tools and come stir up some magic with me.

In a book of this nature, an essential part of the success lies in the contributions of skilled friends and acquaintances and I have been particularly fortunate to have been the recipient of some exciting and colourful illustrations from many dear people to whom I offer my warmest thanks. I could not have shown such a broad view of the wool scene without their generosity and encouragement. Thanks are also due to Alec Dalglish of the Knitting Craft Group, who once again made photographs and published material available to me and whose interest in my work has meant so much to me over the years.

I also gratefully acknowledge the help and cooperation of my publisher and her staff at Search Press who take such an enthusiastic delight in my efforts and allow me to meddle at all stages of production. Not least, a huge thankyou to my husband Keith for his loving support and interest.

Jan Messent.

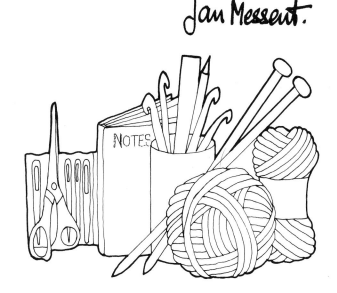

Wool'n sheep

For many people, including myself, the fascination of yarn
begins with the sheep. The sight of those slightly stupid, woolly,
endearing creatures transports us mentally backwards into
the days of our childhood;
to farms, freedom, picnics and wild moorlands,
tufts of wool caught on walls, lambs, shepherds and sheepdogs,
the indignant bleating and the jostling of fleecy backs.

Wool 'n fleece

The sight and sounds of sheep being dipped, sheared, herded and released as though from a catapult are memories which never seem to lose their savour, and any visual or tactile reference to them has helped to retain that appeal, so that the feel of the fleece when spinning, and the smell, too, can take me closer to those memories. Judging by the far-away look on many faces at the merest mention of sheep, I suspect that I am not alone in these feelings, and so I have devoted this first chapter to them, not to an account of the woollen industry, (that can already be found in other books), but simply some interesting facts to do with sheep, wool, work and wear.

Herdwick

Merino

find that British sheep have many times been the mainstay of breeding programmes developed by other countries for their own particular requirements. As Britain's main industry from pre-Roman times was the production of wool, it is not surprising that there are so many different breeds, each of them able to cope so well with the changing geographical conditions of these islands.

One wonders, on looking at old prints of prize animals painted as a record of their fantastic proportions, how the tiny stick-like legs supported the over-sized and unattractive bulk which the proud farmer had bred in order to advertise his prosperity and

Jacob

Whatever our own favourite breed might be, we have to admit that the Merino wins, cloven-hooves down, when it comes to producing wool - not only the most, but the finest, too. This huge beast is a native of Spain, and the type which now produces Australia's most important export is a strain reared since the late 1790's for its exceptional quality and quantity of wool. This is not a fleece for novice spinners to handle as the staple, or the length of the fibres from cut-end to tip, is short and very dense. New Zealand, too, has its super wool-producer in the Corriedale which was bred by crossing the Merino with some English longwools. We

success. Part of the answer lies in the following extracts from the records of Thomas Bewick, the engraver, who was commissioned by a sheep-breeder in the 1800's to make some engravings of his best specimens:

'After I had made my drawings from the fat sheep, I soon saw that they were not approved, but that they were to be made like certain paintings shown to me. I observed to my employer that the paintings bore no resemblance to the animals whose figures I had made my drawings from: and that I would not alter mine to suit the paintings shown to me....I objected to put lumps of fat here and there where I could not see it, at least not as exaggerated a way as the painting before me...'.

Dorset Down

All of this seems to suggest that he was willing to go a little way towards exaggeration but not quite *so* far! Needless to say, Thomas's principles caused him to abandon that particular commission. Some of these monstrous sheep were exhibited in public, being taken from town to town as an advertisement of improved breeding.

Swaledale

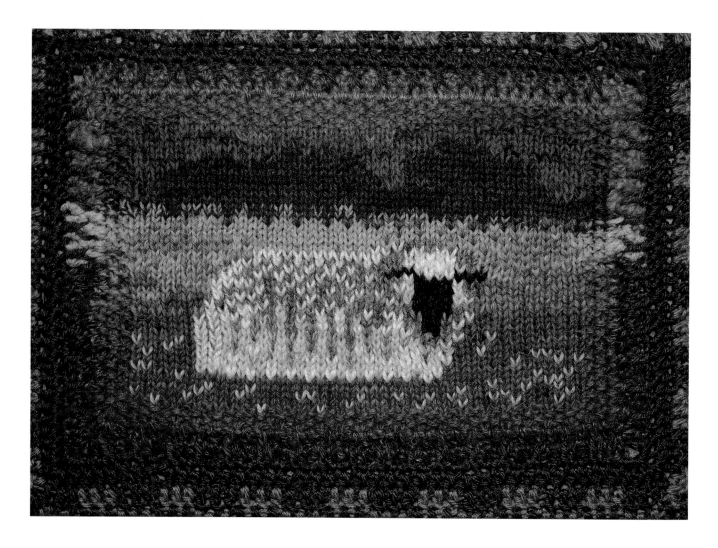

The sheep in the meadow

The knitted central area of this small panel measures 9½ × 6ins/24 × 15cms and is worked in stocking stitch surrounded by a narrow border of moss stitch, and then a border of crochet. Double yarn was used for the knitting, often two different colours together, in order to blend the tones to produce a more lively and interesting effect.

Much use has been made of Swiss darning, an embroidery method by which stitches can be superimposed upon stocking stitch, exactly following the formation of the knitted stitches and having the advantages of both adding details and covering mistakes. The original knitting was much less detailed than the finished product seen here, and I was able by this method to add several details and corrections which did much to improve it. Instructions for Swiss darning can be found in many knitting books, and in my previous book 'Have You Any Wool?'.

Top right
What became of the perm?
*A lino print by **Barbara Robertson** illustrating colours and patterns.*

Bottom right
The knitted Merino – Harry Ram
*By **Sheila Garnett***
A life-sized sheep knitted in garter stitch, showing the sumptuous rolls of wool in true Merino style and the handsome curling horns.

Wool 'n trade

References to the ancient wool trade can still be seen today in churches built at the expense of wealthy merchants, such as the sheep, woolsack and shepherds' crooks which decorate the tomb of one such merchant in Gloucestershire.

*sheep, woolsack and crooks
decorate a merchant's tomb*

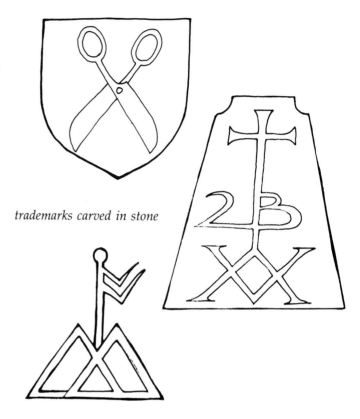

trademarks carved in stone

Coats of arms often show the tools used in some towns, like the cloth-hooks and teasels on the arms of Kendal in Cumbria. Teasels were used to brush up the nap of cloth and also in carders to untangle wool before spinning.

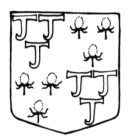

coat of arms

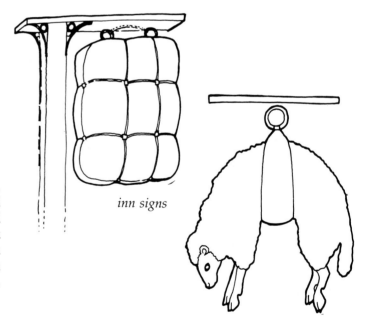

inn signs

The merchants also had symbols, or trade-marks, with which they labelled their property or wares, and these shown here, are carved in stone in the old wool towns of the Cotswolds. The inn-sign of the Woolpack can still be seen in this huge three-dimensional version in Norwich, and the Fleece, is a well-known symbol in many towns where wool was an important industry, both as an inn-sign and on coats of arms.

Wool 'n language

The English language now abounds with phrases reflecting the industry of the middle-ages, when wool and sheep were the main source of income, and where spinning and weaving were the daily occupations of the entire household in many areas. Phrases such as 'dyed in the wool', 'spin a yarn', 'on tenterhooks', and 'a web of lies' are now in common usage, and the 'spinster' was so called because the job of spinning was usually alloted to the unmarried women of the household. Today, all unmarried ladies are known as spinsters, but other names have also been passed on in this way; Fuller, Weaver, Webster, Webber, Webb, Tucker, Walker, Dyer and Lister are all names once connected with the production of woollen cloth.

We can still, of course, see inn signs connected with the old wool trade. Many of them, where wool, money and work were exchanged in days gone by, bear such names as 'The Wool Sack', 'The Packhorse', 'The Staple', 'The Fleece' and 'The Ram', and in the House of Lords in London, the padded bench-seat known as the Woolsack is a permanent reminder of the source of wealth during the time of the early parliaments.

Ancient counting-systems are still employed in some of the more remote sheep farms of the country. Many farmers of today can still remember their ancestors counting the sheep as they dashed through the sorting-gate - 'yan, tan, tethera, pethera, pimp, sethera, lethera, hovera, covera, dik'. Compare these words to the Welsh names shown in brackets - yan (un), tan (dau), tethera (tri), pethera (pedwar), pimp (pump), sethera (chwech), lethera (saith), hovera (wyth), covera (naw), dik (deg).

The shepherd's year is a long round of activity and by no means the romantic occupation suggested by Victorian artists. The shepherd is not only responsible for a valuable flock of wool and meat-producers, but must also attend to their well-being throughout the year. This includes treating their ailments, dipping them to protect them from parasites during the warmer months of the year, attending to mating in the autumn, lambing in the spring, shearing in early summer and then sorting and weeding out the young, male, female and old, castrating and marking, selling and buying in new stock. Terms used to denote various stages of sheeps' growth vary from one part of the country to another, but the most familiar to me are:
Ewe - female sheep.
Ewe lamb - female lamb.
Tup (or ram) - male sheep (a sheep 'tups' when it butts with its head).
Tup lamb - male lamb.
Wether - castrated male bred for meat.
Hogg (or teg) - after five months, or after weaning, a first-year sheep becomes a hogg, (note the two g's).
Gimmer - a female after being shorn for the first time.

Shearling - a male after being shorn for the first time.
Hogg-wool - the first shear and usually the best.
A sheep then becomes known as a 'two-shear', 'three-shear' or 'four-shear', after which her teeth stop growing. When a sheep can no longer graze, she becomes 'broken-mouthed', and is sold for meat.

The manners of sheep

The following poem entitled 'The manners of sheep', was written by the American, John Albee, in May, 1891:

All up and down the greeny grass
The sheep in flocks together pass;
With nibbling noses hills are sewn
And where they go the sod is mown.

With thick-set tails a-wag behind -
They roam or nibble with one mind:
And if one lifts his head on high
All other heads at once up fly.

As stones in field, then stand they still
Or run they all with single will;
And whether there is aught to leap,
All jump if jump the leader sheep.

Where learned the simple sheep such ways
No one had told in ancient days;
But now some think they learned them when
The silly sheep were silly men.

Aran sheep
*A lino print by **Barbara Robertson***
Who better than the sheep himself to wear the traditional Aran garment?

A weaving story

The inhabitants of many towns and villages in England during the 18th century had looms, and earned their daily bread by weaving the wool which had been spun by other cottagers and delivered to them by the 'broggers' on pack-horses. This cottage industry was extremely wide-spread, and hard for all except the wealthy merchants. The following excerpts of one hundred years ago illustrate the point:

'The inhabitants of Ossett, a village three miles from Wakefield, have been employed in making broad woollen cloth from time out of mind. In this year (1734) the weavers, etc., employed in that trade, had to work fifteen hours every day for eightpence. A horn was blown at five o'clock in the morning, the time for beginning, and at eight at night, the time for leaving their work. The clothiers had to take their goods to Leeds to sell, and had to stand in Briggate in all sorts of weather. About the year 1736, Richard Wilson, a resident of Ossett, made two pieces of broad cloth; he carried one of them on his head to Leeds and sold it - the merchant being in want of the fellow piece, he went from Leeds to Ossett, then carried the other piece to Leeds, and then walked to Ossett again; he walked about forty miles that day.'

From 'The Annals and History of Leeds'
compiled by John Mayhall (1860)

'Weaving is a simple job with power looms, and easier; that is all. But, bless me, with hand looms it was horse-work. There are cotton-weavers in Lancashire that think they are punished because they have to stand more nor eight hours in a day and see their work done for them. Why, we thought little in them days of tewing away, week in and week out, for fourteen and fifteen hours, taking our meals where we sat. And even at that, a man that wove in his own house sometimes wrought all night to finish his piece so that he could set off with it at daylight on his shoulder, a tramp of three or four miles over the moor. He brought back, happen, three or four shillings in his pocket, and another warp; and then took his bit of sleep by daylight.'

From 'Web of an Old Weaver'
J. Keighley Snowden (published in 1896)

Nowadays novice spinners often believe that the wool caught in tufts on fences, sharp stones, branches of heather and gates can be gathered in a bag and spun, costing them nothing except the time and energy spent in collecting it. Well, in a sense this is true, but they often do not realise that this is old, broken wool which has been shed naturally by the sheep when, in early summer, the new coat begins to come through underneath. The shed wool is, more often than not, very dirty, brittle and coarse, and not worth the effort of spinning and it is far better, whenever the chance arises, to buy a new fleece from a farmer or a wool-stapler.

If you are keen to learn all you can about spinning, buy a book about it and/or join your nearest branch of The Weavers, Spinners and Dyers Guild who are always eager to welcome new members, whether beginners or not. It is more than likely that there will be fleeces for sale at the meetings, and all the help and advice you can absorb.

As for washing fleece - don't do this *before* you spin it, (unless you are going to dye it first), as you will find it easier to spin in its greasy state. When washing newly-spun yarn, prepare a basin of VERY HOT water and a gentle liquid detergent. Tie the skein, then lower it *gently* into the hot water and leave it there until the water is nearly cold, or overnight. DO NOT AGITATE WHILE IN THE HOT WATER. When the water is cool, gently move the skein about, squeeze very gently then decide whether it needs another wash. If not, rinse it gently several times in lukewarm water, squeeze, *do not wring*, and lay it outside to dry naturally in the open air. Alternatively, let it dry naturally indoors but not near artificial heat. *Remember* - it is a combination of heat, agitation and sudden extremes of temperature which cause wool fibres to shrink and felt.

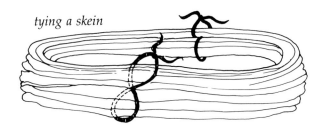

tying a skein

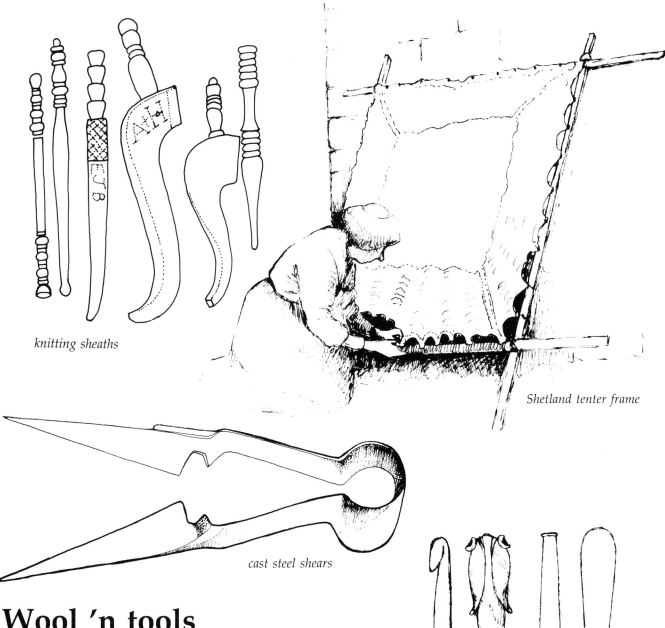

knitting sheaths

Shetland tenter frame

cast steel shears

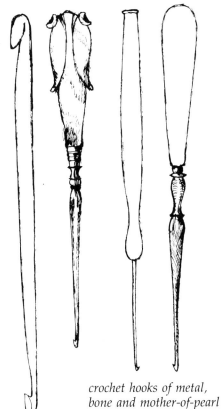

crochet hooks of metal,
bone and mother-of-pearl

Wool 'n tools

Craft devotees now collect old tools connected with knitting, crochet, weaving, sheep and wool. Many of these are nowadays replaced by more modern and sometimes more efficient tools, though rarely more decorative.

Many museums have collections of knitting sheaths like those shown here, which were made of wood and bone and carved by husbands or lovers for the knitters of the family. Each one has a small hole in the top in which to rest the end of the knitting pin, (no knobs in those days), the rest of the sheath being tucked into the waistband, belt or apron-top. This anchored the pin, leaving the other hand free to manipulate the yarn, and so ensure speedier knitting.

Shetland shawls do not display their wonderful lacy effect until they are washed and stretched out to dry on the 'tenter-frame'. This is still done in the same way today, and is regarded as part of the skill of Shetland lace knitting.

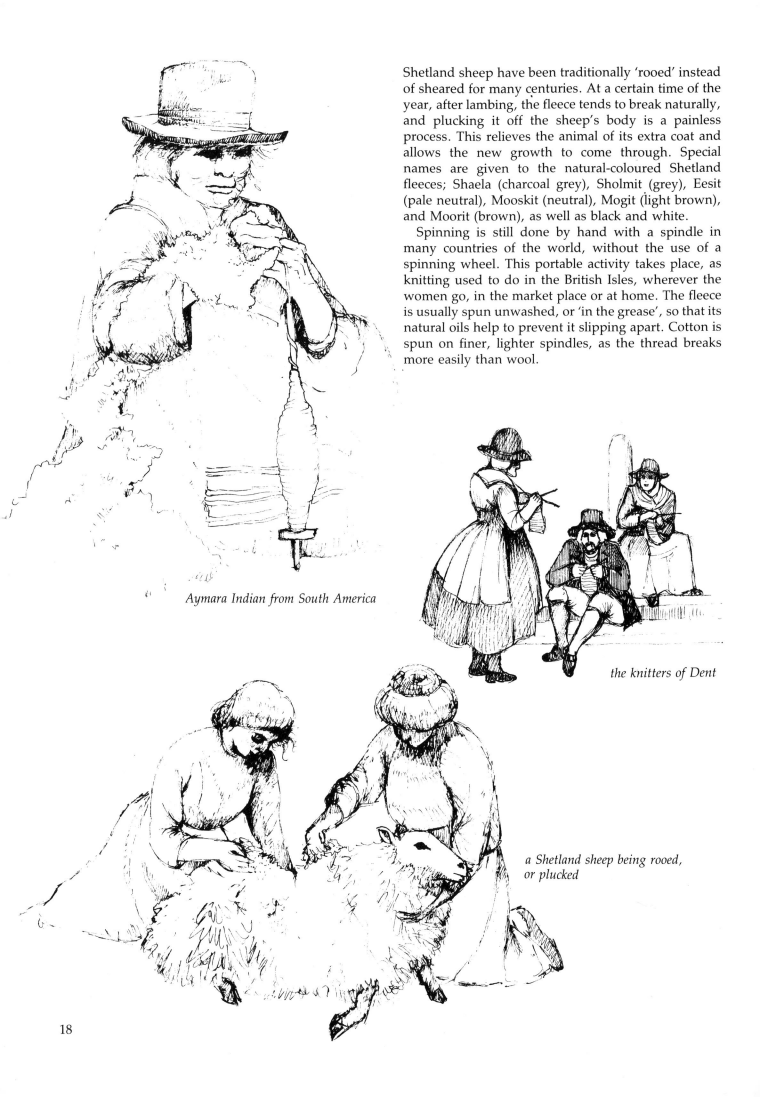

Shetland sheep have been traditionally 'rooed' instead of sheared for many centuries. At a certain time of the year, after lambing, the fleece tends to break naturally, and plucking it off the sheep's body is a painless process. This relieves the animal of its extra coat and allows the new growth to come through. Special names are given to the natural-coloured Shetland fleeces; Shaela (charcoal grey), Sholmit (grey), Eesit (pale neutral), Mooskit (neutral), Mogit (light brown), and Moorit (brown), as well as black and white.

Spinning is still done by hand with a spindle in many countries of the world, without the use of a spinning wheel. This portable activity takes place, as knitting used to do in the British Isles, wherever the women go, in the market place or at home. The fleece is usually spun unwashed, or 'in the grease', so that its natural oils help to prevent it slipping apart. Cotton is spun on finer, lighter spindles, as the thread breaks more easily than wool.

Aymara Indian from South America

the knitters of Dent

a Shetland sheep being rooed, or plucked

Archaeologists have unearthed this statue of a Sumerian King in a common attitude of prayer, in the ancient city of Babylon. He belongs to about 1975 BC and is shown wearing a favourite type of garment made of sheeps' fleece, the tufts shaped into points overlapping each other.

Ancient civilizations in all parts of the world have used the backstrap loom and indeed many still do, for instance, weavers in many parts of South American and in Asia. It is also a favourite method used for teaching children the basic steps of weaving in schools both in Europe and America, as very little equipment is needed, only a few pieces of wooden dowelling, string or cotton warp threads, and a strap to hold the device in place around the waist. Strips of cloth or decorative hangings can be made in this way varying in size from 3 to 18 ins/8 to 46cms wide.

As well as carvings, paintings have added to our knowledge of ancient garments and textile arts, and the walls of many tombs in ancient Egypt illustrate daily occupations, such as weaving. The drawing is a reconstruction of a wall painting in a much simpler style in which the original artist's perspective showed what should be a horizontal loom in a vertical position. We know this by the pegs shown at each end, among other things. Cotton, as well as wool and flax (for linen) were also woven on these simple looms.

Sumeria 1975 B.C.

a backstrap loom

ancient Egyptian horizontal loom

19

The sheep and the landscape box

The background is made of four pieces of card, each one enclosed in knitting, then sewn together. They can bend in both directions. Yards of French knitting were glued on to the background to form the twisted and gnarled trunks, and huge pom-pons, (green on the outside and charcoal/silver on the other), form the tops. These are glued in place.

The tiny sheep were made separately and stuck on with glue. The reverse, (night), side is completely covered with very loose knitting done on huge needles in fine black yarn, and this is mounted over dark blue and black card. Tree shapes can be cut out of white or grey paper and stuck on to the card before the knitting covers it.

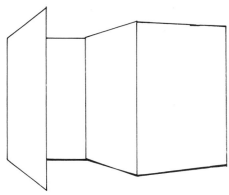

This scenic box opens out to show, on one side, green fields and shady trees made of French knitting and pom-pons. The sheep gather here but at night the reverse side shows the dark sky and tree silhouettes, where the sheep have turned to silver and to sleep, see overleaf.

3-D sheep

The models seen lying down in the landscape are very simple to make.

Materials: 4-ply, (or similar thickness) yarn in sheep colour; size No 12/2¾mm needles; a blunt wool-needle for sewing-up; stiff card for the base; soft padding and one pipe-cleaner for the horns.

Body: loosely cast on 26sts. Knit 2 rows then change to double rib of k2, p2 for 16 rows.

17th row [k2 tog, p2] to last 2 sts, k2 tog, (19 sts).

18th row [p1, k2 tog] to last st, pl, (13 sts).

Work 3 rows in ss beginning with a p row.

22nd row [inc l, p1] to the last st, pl, (19 sts).

23rd row [inc l, p2] to the last st, inc 1, (26 sts).

Begin the next row, p2, k2, and continue in double rib for 16 more rows. Finish with 2 k rows. Cast off.

*base for sheep
seen in landscape*

actual size card

*for use with 4 ply or
finer D.K yarn*

Fold across the centre and sew up the 2 short sides. Gather all round the edge with a running st, pad the shape firmly and slip the card base inside (*Opposite*), lining up the centre mark with the two seams. Pull the gathering thread until the edges just overlap the card, then lace across from side to side to keep the base in position.

Head and neck: using the same yarn and needles, loosely cast on 26 sts and work in rev ss for 4 rows, beg with a k row.
5th row [k2 tog, k4] to the last 2 sts, k2 tog, (21 sts).
6th row p.
7th row [k2 tog, k3] to last 6 sts, k2 tog, k2, k2 tog, (16 sts).
8th row p.
For a different head colour, change yarns here.
9th row k2 tog, k10, turn and p7, turn again, k6, turn and p5, turn and k4, turn and p3, turn and k to the last 2 sts, k2 tog.
For black-faced sheep, change yarns here.
Repeat from the 8th row, (including that row), once more, but do *not* k2 tog at the beginning and end.
Next row p across all sts.
Next row [k2 tog, k2] to last 2 sts, k2 tog, (10 sts).
At this point, if you are using a textured yarn, change to a smooth one for the nose. This is also where the rev ss changes to the smooth side. Also, for black-nosed sheep, change to dark yarn here.

Work 4 rows in ss beginning with a k row, but if a slightly longer nose is preferred, add 2 more rows. Gather the last row up on to a thread and draw up to form the end of the nose, then sew up the head from the nose to the base of the neck. Pad gently and ease into shape. Do *not* over-pad.

Ears: Cast on 4 sts and cast them off again immediately in the usual way. Leave ends long enough to sew the ears to the head as shown. Make two.

Horns: these are made from one pipe-cleaner bent in half and wrapped round tightly with grey or pale-brown yarn. The first end can be wrapped in, but the last end should be threaded through a needle and sewn into the wrapping. Put a tiny dab of glue at the tip of each horn to prevent the yarn from slipping off. Bend the piece to look like the handles of a racing-bike, with a flat part across the centre to fit across the top of the head. This is then stitched in place with double yarn, over and over through the head. For extra neatness, a tiny square of knitting, using the rev side of ss, can be used to cover this area.

To complete: make the eyes with dark (double) yarn in satin st. Attach the head/neck piece to one end of the body. It may be set at a slight angle, or straight on, or high, or low down as in sleep. Sew it carefully all round with small invisible sts.

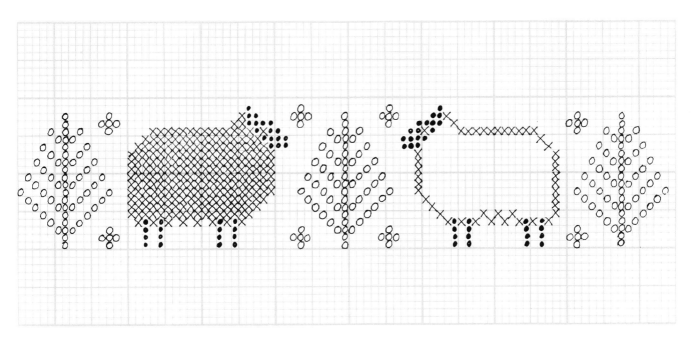

this chart can be used to Swiss darn the outlines of sheep, or for a knitted-in design as part of the landscape panel

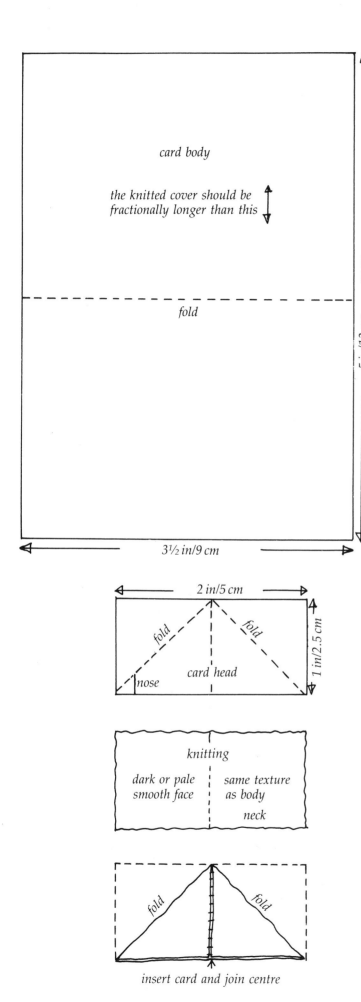

card body

the knitted cover should be fractionally longer than this ↕

5 in/13 cm

3½ in/9 cm

- - - fold - - -

2 in/5 cm

fold   fold

nose

card head

1 in/2.5 cm

knitting

dark or pale
smooth face

same texture
as body

neck

fold   fold

insert card and join centre

Simple 3-D sheep

These instructions can be used as the basis for simple variations of free-standing sheep.

Materials: prepare 2 pieces of thick card, one 5 × 3½ins/13 × 9cms, and the other 2 × 1in/5 × 2.5cms; small amounts of black/grey and white yarns, and the appropriate sized needles.

Body: make a piece of knitted or crocheted fabric exactly the same shape and size as the largest piece of card.
Fold the knitting in half to make a double piece and sew up the short sides to form a pocket.
Fold the card piece in the same way and slip the knitting over this to form a tent-like cover.

Head: make a knitted/crocheted piece exactly the same size as the smaller card, but make one half black and the other half the same colour as the body. Make the face half in ss and the neck half in the same st as the body.
Fold the square as shown in the diagram to make a triangular pocket in which to insert the card when folded. Snip a tiny piece off one corner of the card first to make the nose less sharp, and stick the folded parts down.
Slip the knitted piece over the card and tuck the nose point inside, then sew up from this point to the centre. This shape now sits on top of the body as shown. Sew it in place on each side of the neck. Make the ears and horns as in the first 3-D version (see page 23) and sew them on.
To keep the card body shape open, make a small card wedge and glue this inside, towards the top.

Variations of simple 3-D sheep

1) To make a lying-down sheep, make the card and knitted cover shorter.
2) As above, but use a card (toilet) roll cut down the centre as a base.
3) To make a short-wool sheep with legs, make the knitted body shorter and paint or draw legs on the card.
4) Try various positions for the head, and use different coloured faces.
5) Many different sheep breeds can be suggested using this simple shape; look out for yarns such as mohair and boucles.

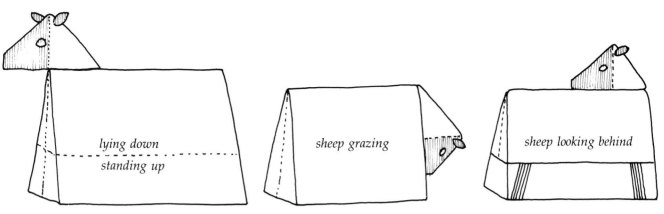

lying down
standing up

sheep grazing

sheep looking behind

Dorset Horn

Black Welsh

Shetland

Hebridean

Soay

Boreray

Herdwick

Southdown

Drawings by **Peter Wilkes**

Shetland sheep
A lino print by **Barbara Robertson**
*This native Scottish sheep sees no reason why humans should
have all the fun! This delightful design was the inspiration
for the embroidery seen below.*

Sheep and stone wall

This small panel, opposite, includes canvas work,
crochet and knitting, both formal and 'free-style' to
suggest the type of limestone scar seen in the Yorkshire
Dales, with a typical dry-stone wall, black-faced sheep
and wind-swept skies. The knitted stones of the wall
are mounted separately on small pieces of card which
are then stuck and sewn on to a background of canvas
embroidery.

The grass is part canvas work velvet stitch and part
crochet loop stitch, (quite indistinguishable from each
other), while the lower limestone area is loosely-
worked free-style crochet, (rather like filet crochet
done with the eyes closed!), using a variety of white,
grey and flecked yarns stretched over white card. The
sheep is made in basically the same way as the
lying-down sheep with the addition of wrapped pipe-
cleaner horns (see page 23).

Shetland sheep
By **Valerie Orr**
*An embroidery made as part of the City and Guilds
Embroidery examination in 1986. Based on the design above,
this interpretation was made mostly in free smocking,
fraying, padding, quilting and machine embroidery.*

Sheep cushion *no written instructions*

This simple cushion is fun to make and has a practical use. Check the size of cushion pad you intend to use and then make a note to adjust the size of each square to fit.

A popular size is 16 × 16ins/40 × 40cms, and for this size each square should measure just over 4in/10cms, allowing for seaming.

Use a separate filling for the head, such as kapok.

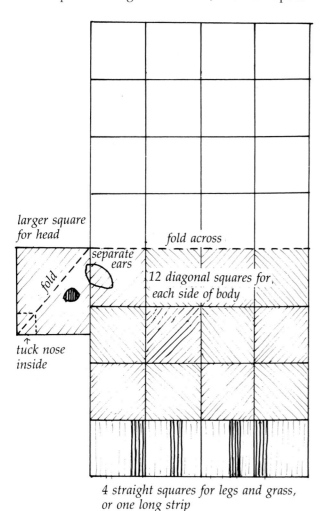

larger square for head

separate ears

fold across

fold

12 diagonal squares for each side of body

↑
tuck nose inside

4 straight squares for legs and grass, or one long strip

The wool bag *no written instructions*

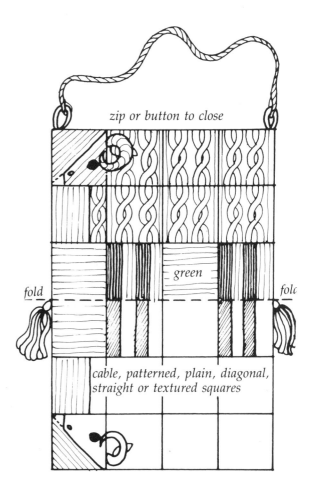

zip or button to close

fold

green

fold

cable, patterned, plain, diagonal, straight or textured squares

28

Wool 'n shapes

Almost any shape can be produced
with knitted or crocheted fabrics. They can be flat,
geometric or random areas of any texture,
or free-standing, three-dimensional models to any size.

Patchwork landscape

Use a variety of different greens, blues and yellows. Some of the trees have extra pieces of lacy knitting sewn over the top; this has the dual purpose of adding more texture and changing the colour.

The sheep are made from tiny rectangles of knitting sewn on top of the panel. You can identify the colours from the chart above.

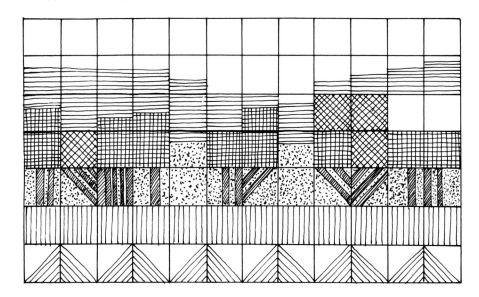

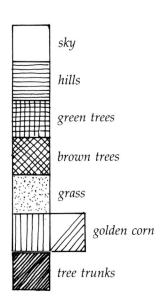

sky

hills

green trees

brown trees

grass

golden corn

tree trunks

30

Knitted patchwork panels

The landscape panels shown on the opposite page and page 33 can be made by anyone who can knit a square. Each panel is made up of 84 small squares measuring 2½ins/6.5cm which are then sewn together to make a rectangle.

Landscape cushion and bed-covers, blankets and even clothes can be made in the same way. The small squares can be made in garter stitch, diagonal garter stitch, stocking stitch or any combination of stitches, (see below), to make interesting patterns and textures.

Materials

Choose No 10/size 3¼mm needles, and yarns which are all of the same thickness. Double knitting yarn was used for these panels, but you can sometimes use two lengths of finer wool if you want to make do with some oddments. You may have to adjust the number of stitches on the needle to make all the squares exactly the same, (especially if several people are working on the same project), as some double knitting qualities are thicker than others.

Panels of this size, (i.e. 17½ × 30ins/44.5 × 91.5cms), may take between 9oz/250gms and 11oz/350gms of yarn, depending on the type of stitches used and the number of applied pieces. Garter stitch uses up more yarn than stocking stitch. It is difficult to estimate how much yarn of any one colour will be needed as this will largely depend on the design, yarn-thickness and so on, but it may help to know that it takes a 2oz/50gm ball of double knitting yarn to make 20 × 2½ins/6.5cms squares in garter stitch.

Colours

You will see from the colour illustration that different blues, greens and yellows have been used for the sky, grass, trees and corn. Mottled, flecked and random-dyed yarns are very useful when working pictorial designs, but you will also need lots of plain colours and plenty of tiny oddments.

When changing colour in the same square, always leave the old and new ends hanging at the back of the work to be darned in later. Also, always have the right side of the work facing you when changing colour, so that the coloured yarns mix together on the back, not the front.

Designing

To design a patchwork panel, you will need some large-squared paper and a spare piece for 'doodling' on, so that you can experiment with shapes. Don't make the design too big for the number of people who will be knitting it, as it takes longer than you might think! Decide how big each square should be and show on your diagram how each one should be knitted.

The pattern base

When the design has been worked out on squared paper, you will need to enlarge it so that each piece of knitting can be pinned on to it as it is made, in order that none of the squares become mixed up or lost. Draw a full-size copy of the design on to brown paper, (see the charts shown on pages 30 and 33), and keep this as the master-plan.

Number of stitches and rows

If this is to be a group project, it would help if each knitter had a piece of card cut *accurately* to size, against which each piece of knitting can be measured as work proceeds. Keep a check on the sizes at all times.

Using size No 10/3¼mm needles and double knitting yarn, you will need about 15 to 16 sts for a stocking stitch or garter stitch square, but this must be checked after a few rows to see that it fits exactly. Remember that more rows are needed for garter stitch than for stocking stitch and you should also allow for the cast-off row to be added into the measurements.

Garter stitch square: every row is knitted and you may need as many as 30 rows. The squares can be placed so that the ridges lie in the opposite direction and all kinds of ideas can be suggested in this way, such as tree-branches, timber houses, fences, windows and doorways.

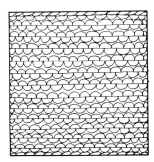

Diagonal garter stitch square: cast on 2 sts and knit one row. On the next row, increase once into each of these two sts to make 4 sts. On the next row, knit. On the next row, increase once into the first and last sts.

Now repeat *these last two rows* until you have enough sts to reach across the square diagonally, then knit one more row. Begin to decrease in the same way until there are only 2 sts left. Cast off, and pull the square gently into shape.

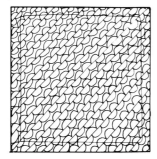

Stocking stitch square: use either the smooth side or the reverse side as the top of the square, or work some reverse rows on to the smooth side to make a ridge.

Making up

Work in sections along the row so that each row can be joined as it is completed. Pressing can be done after all pieces have been joined together.

1) Place two squares RS facing and sew the edges together, as shown in the diagram, with tiny stitches, taking the needle only into the very edges of the knitting. Always use the same yarn which was used to knit one of the squares as the wrong colour will show on the right side.

2) Work along the row, sewing the squares together until the whole row is completed, then do the same with each row until you have seven long strips.

3) Pin each strip to the one below it (RS together) keeping the joins in line, and sew together as before.

4) When all the strips have been sewn together, press the panel very gently under a damp cloth. Stick pins into the corners and through into the ironing-board to hold the pieces in place as you press.

5) The panel should now be laced across a piece of very thick card, hardboard or plywood cut to the same size as the enlarged paper design. Before you begin lacing, however, there are several methods you can use to prevent the corners of the card-mount from poking through the knitting:
   (a) press a piece of iron-on interfacing on to the back of the knitted panel to strengthen it.
   (b) cover the card completely with a piece of fabric before lacing the knitting over it.
   (c) use a thin layer of polyester padding underneath.

6) Before lacing the panel on to the card, a crochet edge can be worked all the way round the panel so that none of the picture disappears on to the other side. One row of trebles should be enough to fold over the edges, but use a matching yarn so that this shows as little as possible on the right side.

7) Use a strong thread and lace across the back from one side to the other, (see below). Place these long stitches close together and gather the corners with small running stitches so that they fit smoothly on the edges.

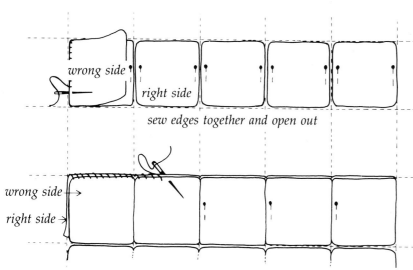

sew edges together and open out

place strips together RS facing, sew edges and open out

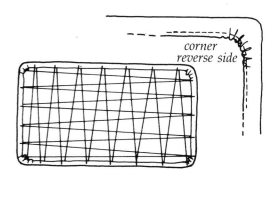

Patchwork townscape

On Sundays and feast days the village people go to church and in winter they wear brightly coloured woollies to keep themselves warm. The inhabitants are small knitted shapes. They were sewn on to the background after it was assembled, as were the church clock and other details.

Note how the squares have been knitted in different directions, some straight, some diagonal and some in a mixture of garter stitch and stocking stitch.

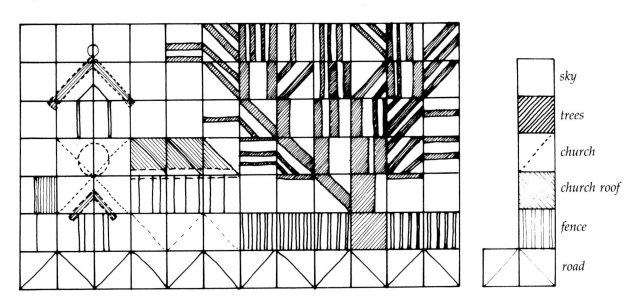

sky

trees

church

church roof

fence

road

Handspun shawl

The wool used to make this large shawl, (see opposite), came from a number of different breeds of sheep, ranging in colour from white to black. These, carded together in different proportions, produce a wide range of tones, and even these can be changed within the hank to give a patchy, graded effect. The yarn is spun on a wheel fairly finely, then two ends are plyed together.

As I nearly always find it easier to cope with small areas and then sew them together, especially on train journeys, this shawl was constructed in a mixture of knitting and crochet from the centre squares outwards. Having sewn the sixteen squares together, it was then just a case of adding more and more round the edge until it looked big enough. About 10oz/300gms of fine 2-ply yarn are needed.

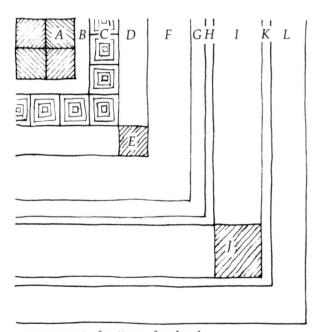

arrangement of patterns for shawl

Stitches used for shawl

A) Knitted diagonal squares.
B) Narrow band of crochet.
C) Crochet ('Afghan') squares.
D) Crochet trebles - several rows.
E) Diagonal squares at each corner.
F) Crochet shell stitch.
G) Two rows filet crochet.
H) Double crochet (dc).
I) Knitted garter stitch.
J) Larger knitted diagonal square.
K) Crochet shell stitch.
L) Crochet trebles - several rows.

The hook size for a light, airy fabric could be as large as 5.50mm or 6.00mm. The diagram below shows only one quarter of the design, but this arrangement is only one possibility, and the design allows for infinite variations. For the wide knitted band, (I), two circular needles were used as rigid ones were not long enough. Push corks or commercial rubber 'needle point protectors' on to one end of each circular needle and use them exactly as you would straight ones.

This shawl was not given a special decorative fancy border, as is always the case with Shetland lace shawls, but if you would like to add one to yours, a very simple pattern in given here for you to make and then sew round the edge. Notice how easy it is to see whether you are on the straight edge or the pointed edge by looking at every alternate row which begins, k3, yo, k2 tog. This is how the straight edge is made at the beginning of the row, while every *other* row, (i.e. the even rows), *ends* with yo, k2 tog, k1.

Diamond shell border

Cast on 12 sts.
1st row k3, yo, k2 tog, k1, (k2 tog, yo) twice, k2.
2nd row k2, yo, k2 tog, yo, k5, yo, k2 tog, k1.
3rd row k3, yo, k2 tog, k4, yo, k2 tog, yo, k2.
4th row k2, yo, k2 tog, yo, k7, yo, k2 tog, k1.
5th row k3, yo, k2 tog, k2 tog, (yo) twice, k2 tog, (yo, k2 tog) twice, yo, k2. Now, k2, turn, and k2 to lengthen edge.
6th row k2, yo, k2 tog, yo, k5, p1, k3, yo, k2 tog, k1.
7th row k3, yo, k2 tog, k2, k2 tog, (yo) twice, k2 tog, (k2 tog, yo) twice, k2.
8th row k1, (k2 tog, yo) twice, k2 tog, k1, p1, k5, yo, k2 tog, k1.
9th row k3, yo, k2 tog, k2 tog, (yo) twice, k2 tog, (k2 tog, yo) twice, k2 tog, k1. Now k2, turn and k2.
10th row k1, (k2 tog, yo) twice, k2 tog, k1, p1, k3, yo, k2 tog, k1.
11th row k3, yo, k2 tog, k2, (k2 tog, yo) twice, k2 tog, k1.
12th row k1, (k2 tog, yo) twice, k2 tog, k3, yo, k2 tog, k1.
Repeat these 12 rows for required length. Cast off.

The soft, muted colours of natural undyed wool enhance the knitted and crocheted textures of this superb shawl.

Crochet reminders

Trebles (tr), symbol Ŧ.
Yarn round hook twice (yrh).
Enter hook into chain space (ch sp).
Yrh and pull through.
Yrh and pull through two loops.
Yrh and pull through two loops to finish.

Half trebles (h tr), symbol T.
Yrh twice.
Enter hook into ch sp.
Yrh and pull through.
Yrh and pull through all 3 loops at the same time.

Double crochet (dc), symbol +.
Enter hook into ch sp.
Yrh and pull through.
Yrh and pull through two loops to finish.

Filet crochet

The basic stitch is simply trebles with a space between each one, the space being replaced by one or two chains. The next row can be worked either:
a) by working the trebles into the ones underneath.
b) or into the chain 'holes' underneath.
The example shown here is the first of these.

Shell pattern

If you make each row in a different colour or tone you will produce waves like those seen in the shawl. You need multiples of 6 sts + 1, and add one extra on to the base chain.

1st row 1dc into 2nd chain from hook, *miss 2ch, 5tr into next ch, miss 2ch, 1dc into next ch,* repeat from * to * to the end.

2nd row 3ch, (this counts as the first tr), 2tr into first st, *miss 2tr, 1dc into next tr, miss 2tr, 5tr into next dc, *repeat from * to *, ending the last repeat with 3tr into last dc, miss out the turning chain, and turn.

3rd row 1ch, 1dc into first st, *miss 2tr, 5tr into next dc, miss 2tr, 1dc into next tr, *repeat from * to *, ending with 1dc on to top of turning chain, and turn.

The last two rows form the pattern.

Look at the diagram of symbols, and follow these as you read through the pattern. It will help you to see what is happening.

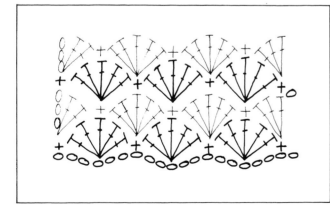

Scottish Islands knitted and designed by *Alec Dalglish*

A knitted panel, (15×9ins/38×23cms), made in 1987, (see above). The card seen on the lower edge shows a reproduction of a painting, ('Sea and Rocks, Iona'), by the Scottish artist S.J. Peploe. The colours used in the knitted panel were all chosen to reproduce, as exactly as possible, those seen in the painting. This usually takes some considerable time, as no matter how many yarns one has from which to choose, there are always more to be added, and for this kind of exercise, these need to be more or less all to the same thickness.

There are no highly-textured yarns in this panel, but where some yarns may be too fine to be used alone, double or even treble thicknesses work perfectly well. This is, in fact, an advantage, as the subtle colour changes which can be introduced by this method are infinitely more interesting than single strands. Over twenty different yarns were used on this panel.

No charting on graph paper is necessary to make a panel like this; the knitting is begun by casting on the requisite number of stitches to fit along the bottom, or side edge, if the design works better that way, and then working several plain rows to start. In this case, an attractive border of single moss stitch has been worked into the design, which not only gives a well-finished appearance but also helps to prevent curling at the bottom and side edges.

To 'read' the design in order to knit it, one must scan it in lines from side to side, beginning at the bottom and working up. The depth of a 'slice' moved upwards on each row depends on the size of the piece, the

proportions, the skill of the knitter and various other factors, such as having the correct colour or being able to manufacture it from those available. One must constantly try to relate the position of shapes to each other, though these are not as important as the colours one chooses, as can be seen in this example. Tones and colours can be 'played down' or exaggerated, according to the choice of the knitter.

One of the most frequent questions asked of 'creative knitters', (for want of a better name), by people to whom all this is new, is, 'Do you just make it up as you go along?' Well, you could answer in the affirmative, which would imply that the whole thing may well be a fairly mindless hit-or-miss operation, something akin to a doodle; or you could answer in the negative, which would imply that it has already been worked out beforehand and you are simply following instructions. Either way gives little credit for the intense effort of concentration needed to knit a panel like this, not to mention the pleasure and sense of achievement. I often wonder whether those people would ask the same question of a painter, an author or a lecturer!

If you look carefully at the panel and painting shown here, you will notice that the knitter has not tried to put the whole of the picture within the frame, and that only the distance and the middle-distance are represented. Being selective is important, and helps to make more things possible to the knitter who might otherwise become discouraged by too complicated a design.

It may help, at first, to draw the general shapes

within a framework which is the same size as the piece you wish to make. Then you will be able to see more easily where you should begin to introduce new shapes, and how many stitches/rows you might need. However, this should not be used as a strict rule to follow, only a beginners' guide, as the colours and their arrangement within the panel are the most important part. The actual source of design is only to be regarded as an aid to a possible arrangement of colours.

The example below shows the designer's inimitable style of knitting and her skill is illustrated in this small sample piece where the subtle blending of colours is clearly seen. Her use of two and three strands of yarn in every stitch, (i.e. double and treble thickness), enables her to give varying degrees of emphasis to any colour by changing one, two or all three strands at any time. This is done by breaking off one strand and tying in another one, so that three strands are in use at all times, though sometimes these may be all of the same colour if that is what is required.

*Sample of coloured knitting by **Margaret Williams***

Ideas for colour stem from diverse sources, whatever fits into the scheme of things at the time. Sometimes this may be an impressionist painting, old oriental carpet patterns or the designer's own pastel sketches of the garden. No charting is done on graph paper before work begins; the knitting is done straight from the design source using 2-ply Shetland wool yarns.

Changing colours in picture knitting

The very small areas of colour required in picture-knitting, (sometimes referred to as 'Jacquard' knitting), pose something of a problem, as sometimes there may be as many as twenty different colours in use along one row. As some of these patches may only consist of no more than a stitch or two in a colour, it is sensible to use short lengths of yarn, rather than keep them attached to the ball, when they easily become entangled with each other.

You may not be able to estimate how much yarn you need for one small area, especially as it may 'speckle' in and out of other colours, so break off no more than one yard/one metre and keep this hanging free, along with all the others on the purl side. When you feel that you need to add more to it, tie another piece on, using a *reef knot* not an overhand knot, and continue. Either knit on through the two loose ends using the yarn double at this point, and through the knot, or leave the ends to be darned in later. If this is to be purely a decorative panel, the ends will not matter unless there is a danger of a hole showing, some unevenness on the surface or bulk beneath the surface. Any tangling can easily be sorted out by gently pulling the lengths of yarn through the rest.

As each new colour is picked up, it should be twisted underneath the one just dropped so that the two yarns 'link arms' and prevent an ugly gap appearing. This should be done at every change and on every row.

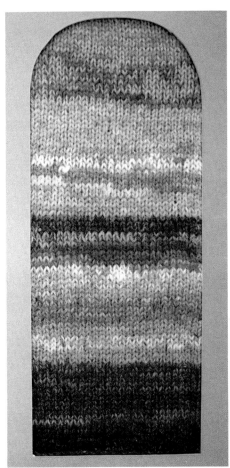

Two small window panels.

These two small panels illustrate a method of designing for picture-knitting without using a painting, photograph or chart as a reference. Behind the curved window-mount, the panel on the left is a rectangle of card around which yarns of different types have been wrapped. This technique is explained in detail in my previous book 'Have You Any Wool?' The yarns are layered from either the lower edge, top or centre to form a simple landscape, and designs can be made in this way in a matter of moments by young and old alike. This is a fascinating project for children.

Once the wrapped design has been approved, the knitted copy can be planned by choosing colours in plain, smooth yarns which match the wrapped panel or will give the same effect when blended. The right-hand panel was knitted in stocking stitch on fine needles with 3-ply Shetland yarns, though any type of yarn will do as well. The colours were chosen to match the wrapped ones on the left as closely as possible, though where this was *not* possible, the stitches were mixed to softly blend the colours together. On such a narrow piece, (only about 3¾ins/9cms wide), it was not difficult to have several colours in use on one row, as only very short lengths were needed.

A particularly interesting development of this exercise is that textured and smooth yarns of the same colour will appear quite different once they are knitted and worked into stitches. This has something to do with the way in which shadows are cast by textured yarns, compared to smooth ones. Shiny yarns reflect the light and appear to be lighter when wrapped as they cast less shadow, and so will be nearer to the true colour than when they are knitted.

This colour change applies to embroidery as well as knitting and crochet, which is why completely different effects can be obtained by changing stitches. Because of this, colour-matching must take place as a continuous process during work, as different lighting conditions can make important changes to colours and tones.

The knitted panel was a rectangular shape to match the wrapped panel; the curve was produced by the card mount. This particular method of mounting by using shaped card stencils can be adapted to many other uses. This knitted panel could be incorporated into the sleeve of a garment, with a continuation of the landscape on the front and back.

The four seasons' panels

The long narrow format of these four panels is very similar to those seen on the previous page, combining both the techniques of wrapping and knitting, and noting that crochet is also included here. The panels were originally made for a trade exhibition, the requirements being that they must be easy enough to carry, put up and take down, and that they must fit into the back of an estate car! So each panel is about 52ins/132cms high and between 9 and 11ins/23 and 28cms wide. The separate pieces of knitting, crochet and wrapping are mounted over a light chip-board, stapled and glued on to the edges and round the back. You will be able to see where the separate wrappings, some with gentle curves, some straight, have been positioned next to patchwork knitting and strips of crochet. Crochet chains have been placed at intervals between some of these pieces, and in each panel the extreme top, (i.e. the distance and sky), was knitted in one piece in stocking stitch, similar to the Scottish Islands on page 37.

Designs for panels of this kind can first be drawn out on paper, just to organise ideas, or even straight on to the backing panel. If the project involves several people, it is probably just as well to draw it first so that everyone knows which bit goes where, and what it is expected to look like. But if one is working alone, so much happens unexpectedly, things change places, ideas get better and sections turned upside down, so there are good reasons why one should just begin and let it evolve. This is not 'leaving it to chance' nor is it called 'making it up as you go along': it is simply doing what artists do, beginning with an idea in the mind (yes, you must have thought about it beforehand to a certain extent while you were collating the material) and then allowing the materials and your imagination to collaborate in harmony together, with your hands in control of the technique.

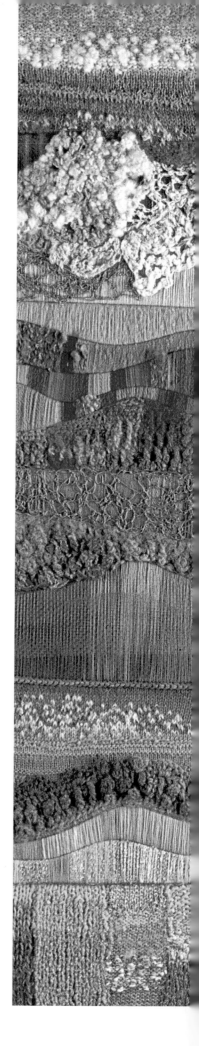

41

Mermaid

The idea of knitting something magical and enchanted has appealed to me for some time; wizards, unicorns, dragons, sparkling costumes and detailed shapes; what problems, what challenges! So Miranda took shape, being one of the easiest to visualise.

Miranda's measurements

Measured in the position as seen in the photograph, Miranda measures 11½ins/29cms from the end of her tail to her elbow. From the top of the head to the elbow, she measures 8ins/20cms.

It is always better to make the body and tail too long rather than too short, as according to legend mermaids are beautiful, long-tailed creatures.

Form

The body-shape was fashioned from strong but pliable wire, and this was then bound with long thin strips of soft padding. Next, she was well wrapped with soft pink yarn to keep the padding in place, to make the body firmer and to shape the contours more precisely.

Unfortunately, it would be quite impossible and pointless to write row-by-row instructions for the knitted skin, as Miranda's was made to fit the exact form which had developed. If I were to try to repeat this for another attempt, the original pattern would be quite useless as my second model would be different. Each 'skin' has to be measured against each individual form, so all I can do is to explain how my version was assembled and hope that this will help you to make one even better. The diagrams will help to show how she looked at various stages.

Arms

These are the easiest part and so they are made first. Beginning at the shoulder, estimate how many stitches will be needed to go round the upper arm at this point. Use a tape-measure to find out the dimensions and then do a tension square with your chosen needle size and yarn to tell you how many stitches you will need. I used a fine pale peach 3-ply yarn, (baby yarn was the perfect colour), together with a fine glitter thread which can be bought on a bobbin, especially for knitting in with other yarns. Size No13/2¼mm needles were used throughout.

Working towards the hands, keep measuring against the arm for the length, then decrease slightly towards the end and draw the last stitches up on to a thread. The long seam should be turned towards the back of the arm and the shoulder edge sewn neatly in place. It is inevitable that the shoulder joins will show and the only remedy is to cover them with something at a later stage.

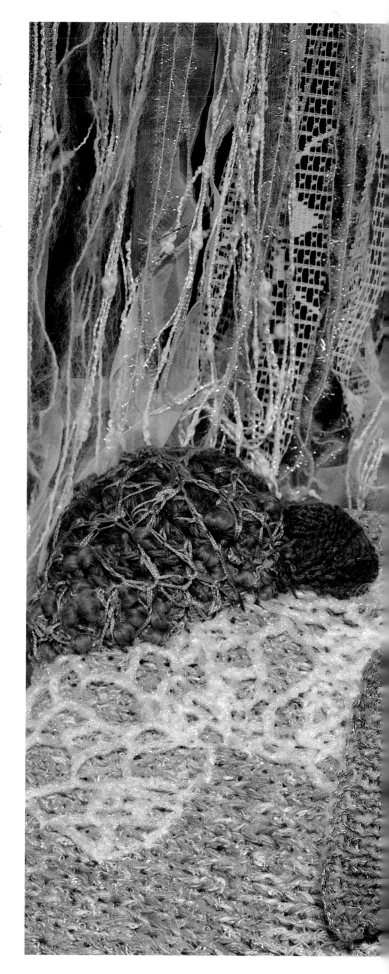

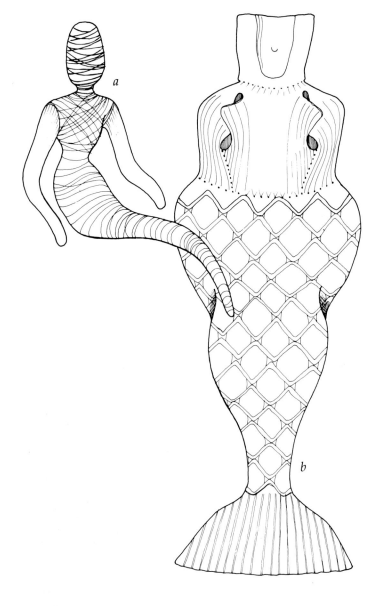

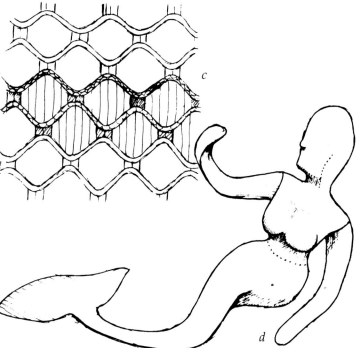

Diagram a) shows Miranda with her arms covered before they were bent into position.

Tail and body

An important element in a project such as this is the correct choice of yarns; correct in the sense that they express the ideas which you have in mind and which compare well with your reference material. There must, for example, be sufficient colours to suggest a subtle change from deeper to lighter tones as the green fish-scales change to flesh. I also used a large range of metallic yarns in different colours. They were used for the reverse stocking stitch ridges in the trellis stitch pattern given below, and were changed continuously all the way up the tail, while the 'ground colour' remained the same, until the top, when it changed to pale green.

The skin was knitted from the tail upwards to the top of the head in one piece. Diagram b) shows what this looked like, with holes made for the arms. The tail fin was worked in double yarn, to make it extra firm, and in single rib to suggest ridges, decreasing at each side towards the narrowest part. At this point, trellis stitch took over, with gradual shaping towards the widest point over the hips. Single, deep-green three-ply with a slight speckle was used for the tail, and metallic yarns.

Trellis stitch pattern for the tail

You will probably need 16 stitches to begin with; after this, increase at each side very gradually, incorporating the extra stitches into the pattern as you go, diagram c). Colour A denotes the background colour, and colour B is the network colour.

With colour A cast on 16 sts.

1st row with colour B, knit.
2nd row knit.
3rd row with colour A, k3, sl 2, k6, sl 2, k3.
4th row p3, sl 2 purlwise, p6, sl 2, p3.
5th and 6th rows repeat rows 3 and 4.
7th row with colour B, knit.
8th row knit.
9th row with colour A, sl 1, k6, sl 2, k6, sl 1.
10th row sl 1, p6, sl 2, p6, sl 1.
11th and 12th rows repeat rows 9 and 10.
These 12 rows form the pattern: begin again at row 1.

Towards the waist, gradually change from deep green to pale green and then to flesh colour, and gradually decrease. Holes should be left for the arms; the shoulder seams are stitched together afterwards.

The face was shaped by part-row knitting and careful padding. The nose and eyes were pulled in and padded out as the head-piece was fitted. There is no need to completely cover the back or top of the head with the flesh-coloured knitting as this will eventually be covered by a knitted hair-piece and plenty of yarn.

The bust area was also padded and quilted by careful stitchery after the skin was sewn in place.

When the skin is complete, it should be pinned on to the body, slipping the arms through the holes and easing the head and face into a smooth shape. Any excess skin can be tucked inside and sewn in! Sew up the back seam very neatly from the right side, slipping the needle under each edge alternately, (you will need both hands for this), with tiny stitches using the colours in their correct sequence. Sew the shoulder seams in place and join the holes neatly to the top of the arms.

A certain amount of modelling must take place to suggest the contours of the face and body. Using a sharp needle and the same coloured yarn, stitch right through the head and body to pull the skin back into shape. Pinch the upper nose and sew this in shape too. Bend the tail and arms into position once the skin is on, diagram d), and make the model balance without falling over. If you feel that the tail fin is too small, make a second larger one and sew this on top, as I did. The join can easily be covered with sequins.

Hair

This is merely a base on to which many lengths of yarn were sewn, diagram e), but it also covers the top and back of the head nicely, and also the back and shoulder seams. I made mine in garter stitch, beginning at one side edge, casting off and on again as shown to make the long, narrow strands.

Part-row knitting at the head-end ensures that this edge stays narrow while fanning out at the other edge. When this is big enough to reach from one side of the head to the other, gather the top edge and sew it into a 'hood'. Slip this on to the head and sew it in place, bringing it well forward on to the face. Yarn for the hair can now be sewn on top of this, long enough to hang right down the back, over the shoulders and into the water.

A close-up of Miranda's features, showing the delicacy which can be achieved with part-row knitting.

45

Decorations and accessories

Extra sparkle and texture can be added to the tail in the form of sequins and beads. The ones I used were in different tones of green, pearl and gold, and were stitched inside each part of the pattern. Palest ones were reserved for the top where the green changes to skin-colour. The trail of seaweed and shells around Miranda's head was made by plaiting textured yarns and sewing many tiny pearls and shells on to it. This was draped around the head and shoulders, and sewn in place. The seaweeds which she holds in her hand are easily made from bunches of crochet chains in assorted green yarns; they are sewn on to the hand and allowed to trail across to the other to cover her lack of real fingers - an omission I regret, but too late!

The face was embroidered with fine stranded cottons. I do not recommend the use of beads for eyes: they are not the correct shape, and do not give the best expression. If in difficulty with this part, use a fine brush to paint these features.

Base

I used a piece of very thick card measuring 17 × 11ins/43.5 × 28cms, over which I laid three separate pieces of knitting and crochet.

Firstly, a roughly rectangular piece of relatively smooth knitted or crocheted fabric to cover the card base completely, with enough extra on each edge to fold round to the back. This is laced in position, diagram f).

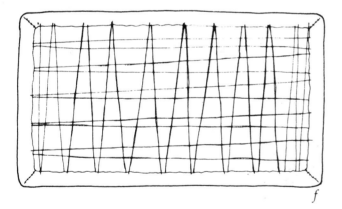

f

For the surf and foam, a large piece of lacy knitted or crocheted fabric is needed. I used a sparkling white yarn on enormous needles, and tried to make as many mistakes as I possibly could! It seemed to work quite well. This is then pulled over the first layer which shows through. Stitch this piece in place.

For the rocks, you need several highly-textured pieces, best made in the free-style knitted/crocheted technique. These can be any shape, but must be large enough to take padding underneath. These are then sewn into place on top of the other pieces. Use a wide variety of yarns for this, to look like rocks, seaweed and algae. Remember, it should look just as convincing as the mermaid, diagram g).

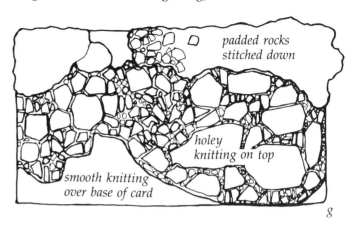

padded rocks
stitched down

holey
knitting on top

smooth knitting
over base of card

g

Decorations for base

Knitted/crocheted fish and shells are not difficult to make, and would add extra interest to an underwater scene. Knitted coral and sea-anemones, (look at books to discover their shapes), boulders and seaweed are also good additions.

Close-up of Miranda's tail.

Wool 'n texture

This chapter is about using the basic skills of both knitting and crochet in unconventional ways to produce effects which cannot be achieved in other yarn techniques. Once the basic stitches of knitting and crochet have been mastered, you will be able to achieve all that this book describes, and much more.

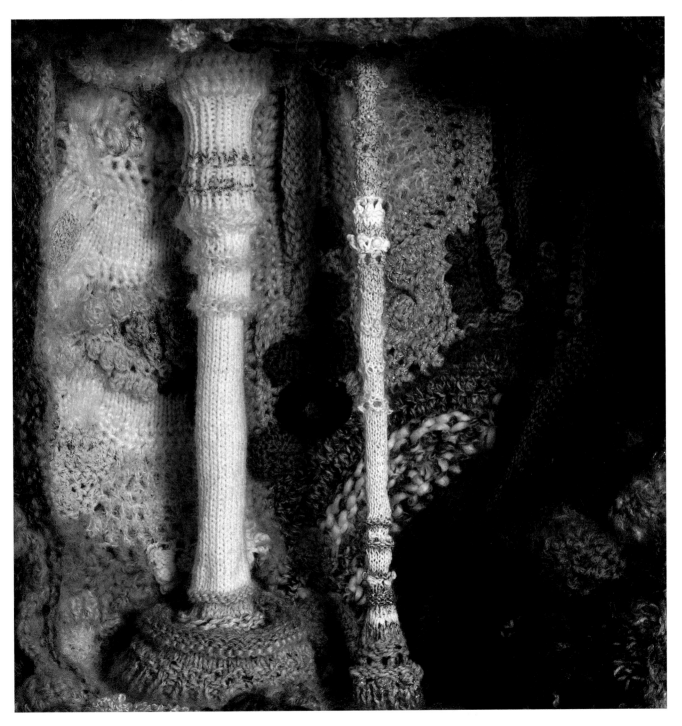

New dimensions

To the experienced knitter and crocheter, many of the suggestions here may sound like heresy, since they advocate the abandonment of all rules and conventions, not as a gimmick, but to open up new ideas and possibilities in hand-made fabric. The usual limitations placed upon hand-knitters and crocheters by shape, wearability, texture, tension and colour are discarded here, as we are concerned mostly with the exploitation of yarn potential, and with having fun. The fabrics constructed *can* be used in a variety of ways, as will be shown later, but this is not our prime concern. For the moment, we will just content ourselves with being artists in yarn.

Note to teachers

The 'having fun with yarn' approach is especially good for teaching young people the skills of knitting and crochet, without the usual emphasis on immediate proficiency. Teach them to knit and crochet on the same piece of fabric, and they will never come to the conclusion that one is more difficult than the other, as many adults have. Instead they will understand the advantages, versatility and limitations of both techniques and be able to use them with equal skill and enjoyment. They will also learn about the properties of many types of yarn, the effects of tension, estimation of yarn and stitch quantities, and all the other various skills which would normally have to be learnt correctly at once.

Here, the word 'mistake' never occurs, as no matter what one does, whether planned or unplanned, the effect is interesting and usually very exciting. The worst that can happen is that not enough use is being made of all the possibilities open to the worker, and not enough variety of yarn, but a look at the following pages should help to remedy that.

In knitting and crocheting new dimensions, every stitch and new direction must be thought out carefully even though the effect you expect may not materialise, and anything you didn't probably will! I have found that this unusual way of working dictates its own results. As I work, I like to think that I am in control of events as I foresee them but, in fact, the fabric often does the most unexpected things just to surprise and delight me, thus secretly robbing me of any credit for the result.

The following maxim should guide all explorers into new dimensions:
Tell me, and I shall forget.
Show me, and I will remember.
Let me do it, and I shall understand.

The basic choices

Even before starting to make a conventional piece of fabric, there are basic choices to be made, such as colour, yarn, needle/hook sizes, stitches and the direction of the fabric. In experimental work, however, these choices will change as the work progresses and as your excitement and involvement grow with it. Decisions about colour, tone, stitch and so on will be made after only a row or two, (sometimes after only a stitch or two), and although the basic choices will be discussed in greater detail further on in the book, they are mentioned briefly here as an introduction.

Colour

For most people, this is usually the first choice as its effect on us is most personal and immediate. To avoid what, to some, may be a problem in deciding which colours to use together, it is often a better idea to choose several tones of *one colour* to make, for example, a scheme of brown tones ranging from the darkest, through rich chestnuts to warm golden browns, beige and neutral.

In a first exercise, avoid contrasting colours altogether, as there is enough to think about, at the beginning, without the possibility of getting this in an unfortunate place.

Yarn

While choosing your colours, you will also be adding variety by your choice of yarn-type, involving both natural and synthetic fibres, (see following pages). This will vary your selection by adding smooth yarns to bumpy ones, hairy, shiny, furry and sparkling ones, *making as much variation in texture as possible.*

Expensive yarns may often be picked up cheaply in sales, shared with friends or left-over from garments, but the real success of the technique lies predominantly with the range of yarns available. In this kind of knitting/crochet, many different types of yarns can be used together, thick and thin, furry or smooth, without worrying about tension, as different tensions produce desirable changes in density and interest. Some types of yarns to look out for are fine 3-plys and embroidery yarns, smooth, shiny and matt rayons and silks, slub wools and acrylics, brushed nylons and mohairs, glitter yarns, crepes, chenille, ribbons, leather, cords and strings, strips of fabric and handspun yarns, plain wools of all kinds, especially random-dyed, (or space-dyed), yarns.

Tools

The word 'tools' refers to either knitting needles or crochet hooks, whichever is being used at the time. The size of tool plays an important part at all stages of fabric construction as this affects the tension, thus producing a variety of different densities and effects. Fine needles for fine threads and thick ones for thick threads are no longer the order of the day; instead, think of the effect you wish to achieve and you will discover, as you experiment, that thick tools and fine threads together produce an open, lacy fabric, while fine tools with thicker threads will make a dense, tight one. It is important to understand that the use of *both knitting needles and crochet hooks on the same piece of work* is essential in order to obtain the greatest possible variety of textures and manoeuvres. So try to have a wide range of sizes available, as you will want to change them often as you progress. The most comfortable ones to use are made of smooth aluminium, not the bendy plastic ones.

Combining knitting and crochet

The combination of knitting and crochet on the same piece of fabric produces unique results. In knitting and crochet, stitch patterns are peculiar to that technique alone, and though some may be similar, most are quite different. For example, there is no stitch in crochet quite as smooth as knitted stocking stitch or as fine as a single moss stitch, and yet crochet *can* produce complicated-looking bumps, bobbles and curves with the greatest ease, which are more time-consuming and difficult to knit.

This means that by combining the techniques on the same fabric twice the potential number of stitches are at the disposal of those who can both knit *and* crochet, even knowing only the simplest stitches.

As you experiment, you will discover the various advantages and disadvantages of both techniques, this being a good reason for introducing this approach to children. How to change from knitting to crochet, and back again, is explained in the following pages and it is also featured in my previous book 'Have You Any Wool?'

Stitches

Having chosen the colour, yarn and tools, you now need to choose a stitch to begin. In experimental crochet and knitting, where stitches can be made in all directions, there is no need to regard your first rows as the bottom, or the last ones as the top. Your cast-on edge may finally be tucked away in the centre, so a neat cast-on edge is no advantage in this case, in fact, a loopy edge is easier to work into at a later stage.

Only the very basic stitches are required to create new dimensions, as the combination of yarns, tools and simple stitches can produce an endless permutation of effects, so much so that it is sometimes difficult to repeat an effect already achieved.

Direction

In conventional fabric construction, the direction is decided at the outset and maintained throughout the garment, or other article. In experimental work, however, new dimensions can be created by the various directions built into the fabric, either by the stitches or by the rows, (see page 52). In knitting, for example, vertical ridges can be made by ribbing, cabling or colour arrangement, while horizontal lines can be made by alternating a smooth stocking stitch with bands of different stitches or by colour-changes.

These are the visual directions of the fabric but there are others.

In crochet, changes in direction are even easier because the fabric is not held rigidly as in knitting, so that turning corners and making strange shapes presents no problems. Knitting or crocheting on to a side edge also creates another direction, even when taken round corners or unevenly shaped edges. Curves *can* be knitted, also wavy lines, simply by employing basic techniques in unusual combinations. You will see illustrations of this further on in the book.

The fabric produced by knitting and crocheting at all angles and in all directions is extremely stable and firm, unless many open areas have been introduced, as would be the case if you were making a cover for a lampshade. The stability of the fabric is due to the small areas of changing direction which pull against each other, preventing sagging or unwanted distortion. This factor makes this technique eminently suitable for garments which never stretch or pull out of shape, even after repeated washing.

Notes on technique

1) There will be no bottom or top to your fabric until you need to decide on this at a later stage in its development. Work grows outwards on all sides like an amoeba.

2) As you work, you can hop about from one side to the other wherever the ideas are developing. There is no need to stay on the same bit.

3) Work only on very small areas of stitches, thinking in terms of *blocks not lines*. Never have more than eight stitches on the go at any one spot, to avoid lines of colour or texture developing.

4) New yarns are tied on every few *stitches* to ensure a mixture of textures and colour-tones. Introduce a new yarn by tying it to the end of the previous one with a firm *reef knot*, leaving long ends of about 3ins/7 cms. These ends are then knitted in (see page 54). Any bits hanging at the back can therefore be chopped off as they should be well anchored in the fabric.

5) Bumps and slubs in textured yarns tend to stay on the far side of the fabric; make use of this by working these yarns from the WS wherever possible, and pushing bumps through to the RS where necessary.

Overleaf
Close-up detail of a rainbow sample.

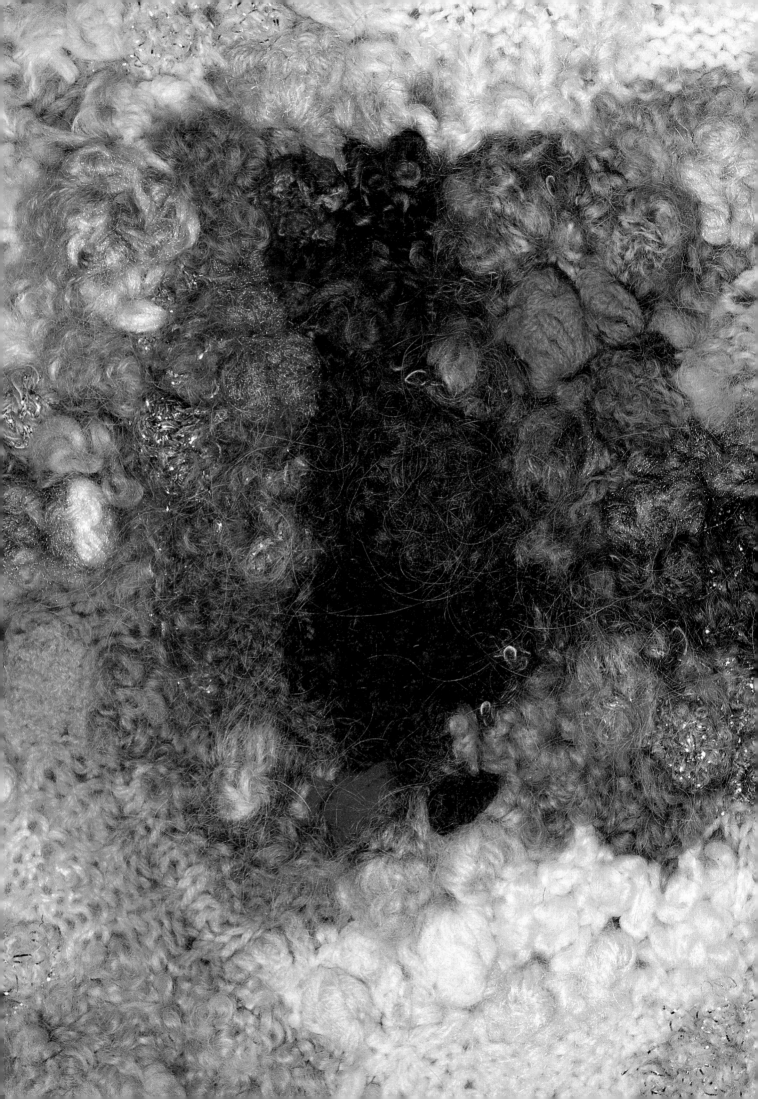

6) Use two or three yarns together for extra colour/texture effects; glitter and metallic yarns are particularly good when worked in this way. Fine yarns can be worked double or with other yarns, and add interesting touches of colour.

7) Increasing and decreasing happens all the time to keep the fabric flat when different yarns and tools do strange things to the tension. Acccept this as part of the technique. They can also be used decoratively to make holes and bumps.

8) Don't bother doing complicated stitches with highly-textured yarns; these will create their own texture, and stitch-patterns will be obliterated to a certain extent. For this reason, choose the technique you find easiest with these yarns.

9) Stitch patterns show best on smooth yarns, and areas of smoothness are just as important and valuable as rough ones, providing a contrast of texture.

10) Change yarns, stitches and tools frequently, and blend them together with care to change emphasis from one tone to another, and from one texture to another.

Changing direction

An experimental sample shown below illustrates the way in which knitting can take various directions, depending partly on the stitch pattern, (ribs and ridges), and partly on the way the work proceeds from a pick-up edge. None of this has been sewn together; it has been picked up from all sides, with some part-row knitting to change direction.

Smooth yarns have been used throughout to make the directional changes more obvious, though normally, a wide variety of different textured yarns would have been introduced to make it more interesting.·

Mixed techniques

Some exciting examples of how to begin experimenting with new dimensions in knitting and crochet are shown on this page.

The example above shows how blocks of knitting are mixed with blocks of crochet. Both textured and smooth yarns have been used. △

Mixed textures

This example shows a variety of different textures produced by a combination of fancy yarns *and* stitches in knitting and crochet. Glitter yarn in open crochet, bumps in a crispy cotton bouclé, garter stitch and picot holes, furry mohair, a thick chenille and smooth ribbing. △

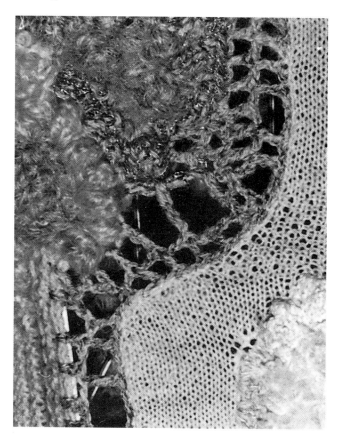

Mixed densities

This example shows a small detail from a lampshade cover made from many white/cream yarns. The areas of openwork (in crochet) allow the light to shine through, as it also does through the finer parts of knitted stocking stitch. Smaller areas of denser crochet and highly-textured stitches provide an interesting contrast which is seen at its best in daylight. ▷

A first experiment

Now for a taste of the action! Try the following experiment but note that a *set of instructions* is not possible with this technique, (too many factors are variable), but only a kind of basic recipe which you can elaborate upon in any way you wish.

Guidelines

Any of the following suggestions may be combined in whatever way you wish but remember that if you have accumulated more than eight stitches, you must find some way of reducing them.

1) Method of preparing the yarn for *the initial sample only*, noting that normally we make our choices as we go along, not all at the beginning, as in this case.

   From at least 12 different types of yarn, but all from one colour family, cut lengths of about 12ins/ 30cms. Now tie these together, end to end, to form one continuous length, using a *reef knot* and leaving ends of about 3ins/7cms, (see below). Try to arrange them so that the textures and colour-tones change gradually rather than abruptly. Now use this as one ball of yarn.

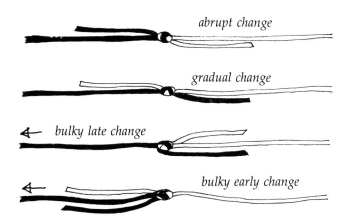

abrupt change

gradual change

bulky late change

bulky early change

lay the loose ends along the working yarn in any of these ways and work them into the stitches; the method you choose will help colours to merge or stay separate.

2) Use any size knitting needles and cast on about 6 sts, then work about 6 rows in any stitch. Cast off all except 2 sts. Point the needle down the side of the piece and pick up 6, 8 or fewer stitches from the side edge.

3) Knit (or purl) about 2 - 3 rows then decrease in any way you like, to one st and keep this one on the needle. Pick up more sts from any adjacent edge and work for a few rows. (If you are working all the ends in as you should, there will not be a RS or a WS at this stage. You can decide on that later.)

4) Now cast off loosely with knitting needles or a crochet hook. Change techniques from knitting to crochet. Using any hook, begin to crochet into the nearest edge using a textured stitch, either dense, bumpy or lacy, depending on the yarn which has presented itself. Make a small block of this stitch - don't go all round the edge - and as soon as the yarn changes again, change tools, *and* the stitch, *and* the direction. Are you getting the hang of it?

5) When your length of yarn has run out, you are free to choose which one to add next, as and when the need arises, not as before, in a random length but making a more careful selection, one at a time.

6) You may now wish to work on one of the other edges, so the following unorthodox ways of proceeding to create texture will help, but remember that there is *no such thing as a mistake*. If you are inclined to ask, 'Am I allowed to ....?' the answer will invariably be, 'Yes. Try it and see what happens.'

Pick up stitches

a) from the cast-on or base chain, and work in the opposite direction.
b) down the side edge of the fabric, and work sideways.
c) in crochet from a knitted edge and vice-versa.
d) from behind or in front on rows below to make a pleat.

Make long stitches

a) in knitting, by throwing the yarn several times around the needle and knitting only one of these loops on the way back.
b) in crochet, triple trebles by winding the yarn 3 times around the hook. Alternate these with short stitches for greater effect.

Make holes

a) by dropping stitches to make ladders.
b) by casting off, then on again in later rows.
c) by leaving some stitches on a pin and knitting the two halves separately, then join across the top.
d) in crochet, miss several spaces, then make a tall stitch.
e) by using jumbo-size needles or hook, with a fine yarn.

Tighten up the fabric

a) by decreasing drastically, 3 or 4 sts into one st.
b) by changing to a much finer hook or needles.
c) by ribbing and cabling, and decreasing at the same time.
d) by changing from a strong horizontal pattern to a strong vertical pattern, e.g. from g st ridges to ribbing.

Stalactite cave
Detail showing part of the centre portion of a large, open-fronted box in which rocks,
stalactites and stalagmites are knitted and crocheted in a wide variety of yarns. The
basis of this construction is wood, chicken-wire and much padding, with wooden
dowels to hold some of the pieces in position.

Make bumps and bobbles

a) by crocheting many stitches on top of each other.
b) by knitting backwards and forwards on the same few sts.
c) by adding small crochet cups or domes.
d) by using a bumpy yarn, or two together.
e) by crocheting very tall and very short sts alternately.
f) by using a cable needle to hold some sts away from the knitting. Then make a long strip with these and twist it before putting the sts back on to the needle.

Make loops and fur textures

Refresh your memory by referring to a book of stitch patterns.
Bias knitting, and surface chaining, (to make rambling lines).
Simple stitch patterns in both knitting and crochet.
Part-row knitting, in which only part of a row is knitted before turning back to the beginning. Try it and see what happens.

Check on your textures and tones

Have you put smooth yarns next to bumpy or hairy ones?
Have you included fine stitches to contrast with the coarse ones?
Have you made some lacy areas as well as dense ones?
Is your sample moving in all directions, or only one?
Are your colour-tones merging gently into each other, or is your sample too contrasty/monotonous?
Are you referring constantly to the five choices: colour, yarn, tool, stitch and direction?

Keeping the fabric flat

'With all these changes in yarn, direction, stitch and tension, how do I manage to produce a flat piece of fabric?', you ask. Well, every now and again, you must put the piece down on a flat surface and see what effects your efforts are having on it.

If it looks as though it may become cup-shaped before too long, you must compensate by relaxing some of the stitches, a) by making a more open texture, or b) by making more stitches available to work on at the point where the tension is greatest.

Increasing and decreasing, as mentioned previously, are part of the process; they shape the fabric as well as create textures on it, so learn as many ways in both knitting and crochet, orthodox and unorthodox, as you can.

What does it look like?

At all costs, avoid the temptation to make your sample look like something, a bird, a fish, a tree. This is an exercise in colour and texture, rather like an abstract painting, done to find out how the process works. At this point, you'll be completely on the wrong tack if you try to paint a 'yarn picture' so keep your mind on the mechanics!

Changing from knitting to crochet and vice-versa

This is easy; simply cast off loosely, (or use a crochet hook to cast off with), and then push the hook into the edge of the knitting, yarn-over, pull through, yarn-over again and pull through two loops. Repeat this, and you are crocheting. It is often useful to leave the last cast-off stitch to be slipped on to the crochet hook as the first loop, using the same yarn to begin crocheting so that the change over is not so abrupt.

To knit into crochet, simply use the chained edge as potential stitches, and pick them up with the point of the knitting needle, yarn-over point, and pull through to the right side on the needle. Remember though, that a ridge will form on the side of the fabric furthest away from you, so if you do not want this to show, do the picking up from the RS and, preferably, with the same yarn as the crochet to avoid a hard edge of colour appearing at that point.

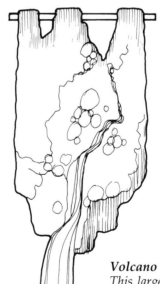

Volcano hanging
This large hanging began in the centre and grew outwards towards the edges. The fiery oranges and hot reds were meant to resemble pictures of molten lava flowing from a volcano and pouring through cooler rock, steaming along the edges. The molten stream at the bottom hangs down further than shown in the photograph, about double the length of the visible area, (see diagram). The meandering line on the right is made by surface chaining.

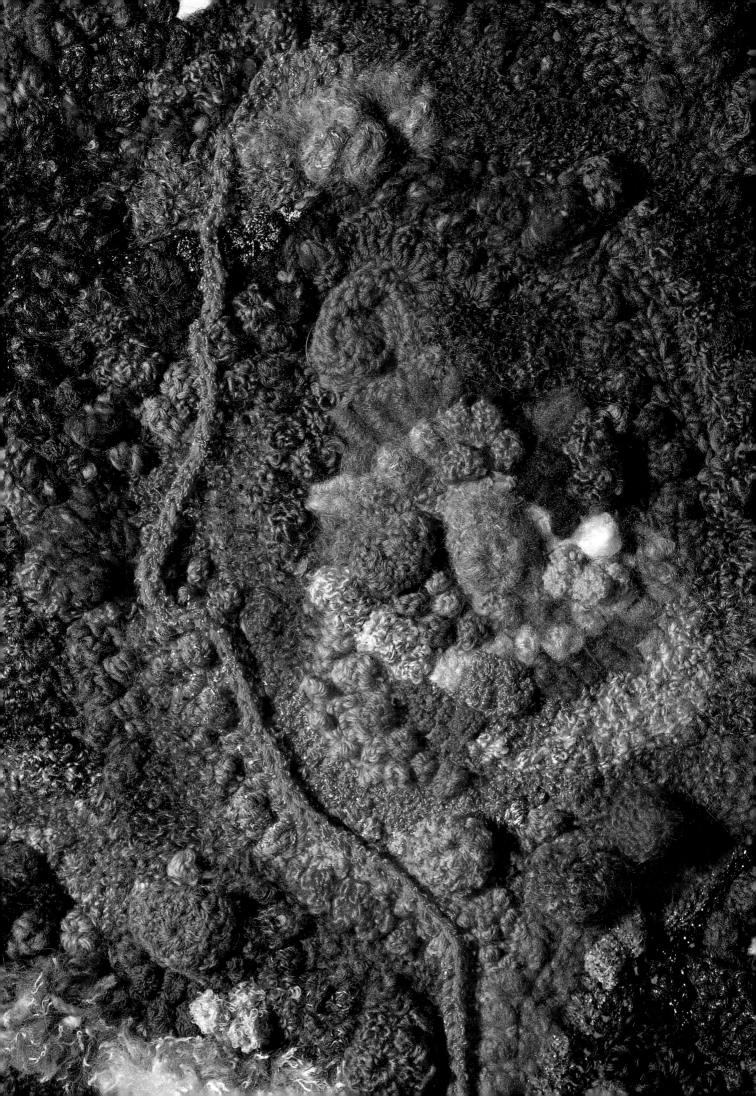

Crochet stitches are bigger than knitting stitches

Crochet stitches are fatter and longer than knitting stitches, so it is to be expected that the tensions will not be the same as you change from one technique to the other. On your sample, experiment to learn how to cope with this, (it is not a problem, only an interesting side-effect), and use it to your advantage.

You can do any, or all, of the following; change needles, change the hook, change yarns, or the stitch, or the number of stitches to a greater or smaller number.

To insert a piece into an angle

Quite often, little angles and 'bays' appear which need to be filled, presenting the problem of how to fix a new addition to two adjacent sides at the same time. One easy way would be to sew a piece in, either on one or both sides, but it is equally easy to knit/crochet it on.

Decide which of the two, (or three), edges you want to pick up stitches from, and proceed as follows:

As the point of the needle reaches the second part of the angle, (i.e. on every other row), pick up a stitch from this edge and, at the beginning of the next row, decrease one stitch to regain the original number. If the slope of the angle is more gradual, you may not need to decrease at all, but keep the extra stitches on the needle to fill the space, but don't allow too many on the needle, (see below).

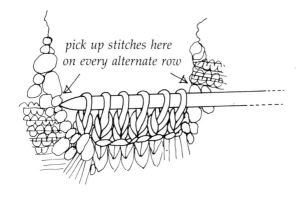

pick up stitches here on every alternate row

If you are picking up extra stitches from *both* sides, as in a bay, do this at the end of every row, and decrease as before if necessary. The same method is used in crochet, but fewer rows will be needed as the stitches are taller. A slip stitch is used to link the worked piece to the sides.

Ideas for texture

It is a happy coincidence that many of nature's textures, (and patterns too), can be successfully re-created in knitting and crochet. Look around at wood, bark, underwater photographs and rocky pools with seaweed, pebbles and rocks, lichen and fungi, foliage and blossom on trees.

If you can, make a collection of ideas under this heading and keep them in a scrap-book. Take photographs and make sketches, and try to reproduce them in this knitting/crochet combination as an exercise.

The all-white sample, above, shows a combination of textures on a flat decorative panel. Wrapped card strips form smooth ridges between lines of textured knitting, and separate padded pieces lower down resemble pebbles on tufted grass.

The effect of smooth and textured yarns, opposite, shows in this sample knitted in rows with ridges and picot holes. It began with the twisted metallic ridge towards the top, then white picot holes were knitted on in the other direction. The twisted effect was obtained by allowing the cast-on stitches to remain twisted round the needle and knitting the first row while they were in this position.

An all-green sample in smooth and textured yarns knitted in stocking stitch, ribbing and moss stitch. The huge bobbles are made in the traditional 'bobble stitch' method, but greatly exaggerated and in different yarns. Compare the result with the tree-bark photograph shown above. This is a perfect example of how art can be made to imitate nature to achieve startling results.

The example, opposite top, shows how double-sided pockets can be padded before being closed up again, to resemble small pebbles, rocks or boulders. Double-sided knitting makes use of the slip-stitch method (refer to Mary Thomas' Knitting Book for details of this technique) and can be incorporated into hangings so that the actual pebbles may be enclosed with knitting, adding even more texture to knitted and crocheted stitches.

The example, opposite below, shows ridges and pleats made on a background of smooth and slub yarns, part-row knitting in mohair, and stocking stitch 'bells' made separately and sewn on in clusters. Additional small shapes may also be sewn on for extra textural effect, or to cover up parts which were not quite so successful.

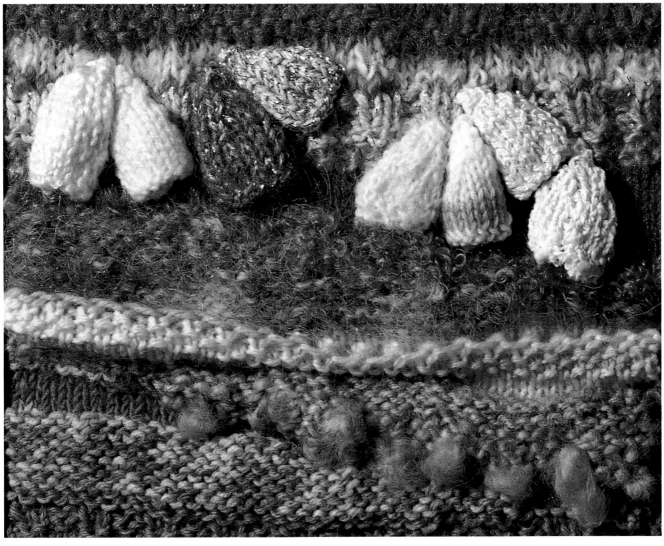

Two cushions, both about 16ins/41cms square, are covered with knitted/crocheted fabric made to represent lichen patches, (left), and tree bark (right).

The whitish, circular, crusty lichen is enhanced by tiny cup-shapes lined with velvety-brown and crinkled frills of browny-greys gather around the edges. Many of these extras are made separately and sewn on to the background of textured whites and browns. Dome and cup shapes are very easy to make in crochet; see my previous book 'Have You Any Wool?' for how to do this.

The tree-bark cushion has more knitting than many of the other pieces, as the high ridges and pleats are made to buckle when the fabric expands, (on large needles), and contracts, (on finer ones). To exaggerate this effect, the stitches can be increased, thicker yarn can be used *and* thicker needles, then if finer needles are used after this with finer yarns and fewer stitches the fabric will pleat, bulge and buckle.

Instead of allowing these bulges to lay in a straight line they can be manoeuvred into curves or pushed up into different positions by pulling the stitches out of line with a crochet hook. Just cast off the stitches and crochet into the cast-off edge, but instead of working an even row, as one would normally do, allow the hook to do unorthodox things which will pull the line of fabric out of shape and contort it into curves.

Lichen and tree bark cushions

Grassy cushion

This cushion is mostly crochet, and simulates rocky patches of earth with tufts of grass and foliage. Domes have again been used, as they are easy to make in this technique, as is also the fur stitch which perfectly resembles grass. Many different greens are used, as one alone would not be convincing, real grass being a combination of very many colours and tones.

It is important to remember this factor as it can make a great difference to a subject's realism; so many good designs are spoilt by the use of technicolour emerald green instead of the real grass greens seen in nature. One may even have to resort to dyeing one's own greens at home for these purposes, as the correct greens are difficult to find among commercial yarns. I have been doing this for some time now and find that it is the only way to overcome the problem.

Gold cushion

Shown below and overleaf, is a detail from a cushion. The colours and textures were inspired by a photograph of veins of gold trickling through a solid mass of surrounding minerals, a feast of grey-blue and sparkling chunks of rock here and there accentuated by black and opaque white.

Minerals are excellent subjects for knitting as the colours, shapes, lines and textures can often be 'read' as lines of stitches and yarn. On the photograph, where colours and textures lost their sharpness and appeared to fade into each other, I discovered that mohair yarn reproduced this effect quite perfectly, the hairy quality disguising the outline of the shape. Metallic yarns were also very useful here, used alone or with plainer ones, and knitted ribbing worked in all directions seemed to suggest the many directions of the rocks as they were compressed into a solid mass.

The strong gold line which worms its way down through the centre was crochet-chained on top of the surface at a later stage to make visual links from one gold patch to another.

Wool 'n colour

To many people, the use of colour creates quite a problem,
and yet the truth is that one can learn how to use it in
much the same way that one can develop any skill -
by trial and error. It is also largely a matter of personal taste,
as with spices and herbs in recipes, for instance.

Experimenting with colour

One good way of choosing colours is to base a scheme on a favourite ball of random-dyed yarn, containing a selection of particularly well-matched tones. Pick out and identify the tiny specks of colour in the ball, using your own yarn supply to do this, and then knit or crochet a swatch in these colours, first using them in the same proportions as those in the ball and then in changed proportions to see what effect this has.

As you will see by the example shown opposite, the colours have been made to move very gradually into each other without sudden changes or contrasting tones. This is done by using two colours together, (i.e. double yarn), and then changing only one of these two yarns at a time as explained in the diagram, (see opposite, below).

Tones of colour which belong to one section of the colour-wheel are known as 'analogous' colours. They are safe and harmonious and can always be relied on to go well together, which is why many people use this scheme in their clothing.

The colours seen in the pink box, below, are examples of an analogous scheme; pinks and mauves with an undertone of grey. The *tones* are decided by the amount of darkness or lightness in each colour, and learning to recognise this is something which takes a little practice, especially when some colours, at first glance, look no lighter or darker than others. This is even more difficult when the colours you are trying to arrange tonally are from different parts of the colour-wheel as some colours are naturally darker in tone than others.

Yarns and threads of all kinds also have their extra problems, as the fibres reflect light in a different way from paint, and shiny fibres can give the appearance of a much lighter colour in the ball or hank than when knitted or crocheted. This is because the stitches have depth which cast shadows, (in embroidery too), and the deeper and more textured the stitch, the deeper the shadow and the darker the tone.

Try to take this into account when matching colours; it helps to do this in good daylight conditions too, as artifical light can make a great deal of difference to both tones and actual colours. It will often be found that two identical tones in different yarns will look quite different when they are used in stitchery of any kind.

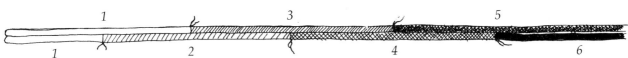

two or more strands of yarn

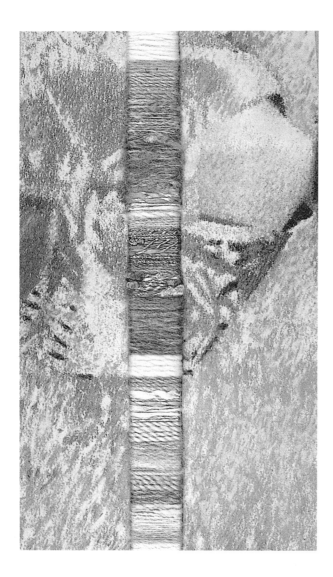

Blending colours

Another useful exercise in colour matching is shown above. The soft pastel tones in an advertisement for perfume were identified in various yarns, (knitting as well as embroidery), and wrapped around a narrow strip of card to isolate them. They were arranged in more or less the same order as they appeared in the illustration, which is why they appear to blend into the background so well in parts.

Having done this, the next exercise shows an attempt to use both knitting and wrapping with the same yarns, blending the colours and tones together in different ways, one by using double yarns, (as previously described), and also by a small counter-change pattern. Random-dyed threads also have the effect of blending several colours together.

The colour-proportions were changed in this exercise, predominance being given to the yellowy-greens rather than the mauves, though several more examples could easily be made by changing the tones around yet again in different proportions, making use of crochet and canvaswork stitches, or working the complete piece in knitted stocking stitch.

The knitted strips were also mounted over card pieces and a re-arrangement of the pieces would have resulted in quite a different appearance to the design.

Working with colour

The colours you choose to work with will depend on the type of experiment you have in mind. If this is totally abstract the choice will be easier, (from a specific yarn point of view), but if you prefer to represent the true colours of, for example, a landscape, rock formation or tree bark, then finding *exactly* the right tones will be more time consuming and sometimes quite difficult. In any case, it helps to begin your collection of yarns immediately by picking up yarn bargains wherever they can be found. Never throw away any oddments, however small, or refuse gifts from friends, however strange the colour, for even these are sure to be useful at some stage.

Always keep yarns clean and tidy in separate containers according to colour; being methodical about this actually helps when you come to assemble colours for a project, (see below).

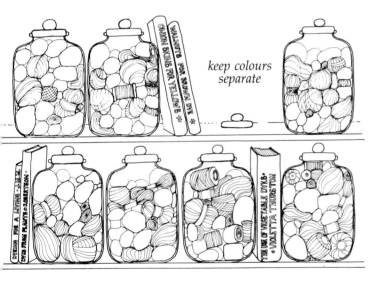

keep colours separate

A colour pattern experiment

As an interesting way of experimenting with colours which may be outside your usual day-to-day experience, try this exercise, guaranteed to produce exciting and unusual effects.

1) First find a full-page magazine photograph, (which you are allowed to remove!), illustrating colours you would like to use. Try to find colours which are outside your usual favourite range.
2) Carefully remove the page and cut it into strips varying from ½-¾ins/1–2cms wide. Divide them into two equal piles and mix them up.

3) Take a large piece of paper and stick double-sided sticky tape along one edge. Remove the backing to expose the second sticky side and place the extreme tips of the cut paper pieces along this, side by side and close together. Use only one pile for this.
4) With the second pile, take one at a time and weave these under and over the first set, pushing them towards the stuck ends to make a woven paper mat. You will see that the colours are now mixing in a completely different way from the original picture, to form an abstract pattern of squares. When all the strips are used up, stick the ends down firmly.

This forms the basis of the experiment, but two more developments are as follows. Using one of the stencils shown on page 125, place this over your woven mat to make an instant design for a jumper. You may even like to knit or crochet a sample piece in the same colours.

Cut a card square frame like the one in the photograph, (see above) and yarn-wrap it in the same colours as the woven paper, trying to match the colours on the frame with those on either its inside or outside adjacent areas. Those on this sample were matched on the inside. This is a good colour identification exercise and helps one to look more closely at colour combinations.

The little knitted square in the centre uses the same coloured yarns as for the frame. It is mounted over padded card and glued in place.

Colour selection

Before you begin, sort out all the colours you want to use on your experimental project, bearing in mind that there should be;

a) A predominance of one main colour.

b) As much variation in yarn-types as possible.

c) Keep contrasting colours to a minimum, to control the colour balance.

d) Cover as wide a range of tones as possible within one colour, e.g. cream, lemon, bright yellow, golden yellow, mustard, brown/yellow. Include random-dyed and marled yarns and mixtures of yellow and white, gold lurex and speckled yarns too.

Change yarns in mid-row, mid-stitch, and often

Change the colour tones more gradually as you work by using two different tones of yarns together, (i.e. double yarn), then break one off and tie in a deeper tone, continue for a row/stitch or two then break off the first one and tie in a still deeper tone, thus changing only one of the yarns at a time. This is a more subtle way of moving through the various tones than by changing yarns completely and abruptly, although there *are* times when this is required.

Place contrasting colours and tones, also black and

white, with great care as they will attract more attention than tones which blend. They should only be placed where you *wish* attention to be concentrated. This also applies to glitter yarns and those yarns which have a contrasting colour built into them. If the contrasting part is unwanted in the place where it would occur naturally, cut it out and rejoin the two ends together. Don't throw it away, though, it may be just what you need for another purpose!

Small areas of colour, as well as stitch-patterns, are a useful addition to experimental pieces. These will also attract attention to themselves and so should be placed with great care.

Swiss-darning is a good way of adding coloured stitches on top of stocking stitch, especially for very small areas.

Crochet chaining adds lines of colour wherever it is needed on either knitting or crochet. Meandering lines are easy using this method, but are best added at a later stage rather than too soon.

Random-dyed, marled and multi-coloured yarns produce irregular and unusual effects when used together with stitch-patterns and lacy stitches, although this goes completely against all the rules. They also look good when used in Jacquard patterns, though here we are speaking of experimental free-style work, not for complete garments. The clarity of the pattern will be lost, but the effect will still be exciting when seen in context amongst other textures.

Contrary to the general line of thought that colour theory may be rather dull and academic, an understanding of the basic principles can be of great help to those whose creativity depends on using colour cleverly and imaginatively. Use paints, coloured pencils or yarn to create your own colour-wheel, and wrap strips of card in graded tones of one colour to experience the discipline of deciding their order. Begin to notice colour everywhere, not only the obvious examples which demand attention by their brilliance but the subtle and more elusive ones too, in nature, in buildings and old brickwork, in people's faces and in the seasons. Look also at paint shade-cards, cut these up and play with the samples. Keep advertisements which appeal to you for their colour, and garden catalogues, postcards, photographs and especially paintings, stained glassware and windows, ceramics, butterflies, shells, shop-window displays and the shelves of yarn shops. Begin to take notice of what people are wearing and how they put their colours together. Be critical of the colour schemes you see, and try to determine the thinking behind them. Ask yourself what you would do in the same circumstances, and then ask yourself why? Demand an answer!

For handspinners, either using a spindle or a wheel, the opportunity arises to create beautiful coloured yarns to whatever specification they require. The operation is somewhat lengthy, but to those who enjoy all the various aspects of handling wool and producing lovely yarns, the time element is part of the ritual to be savoured. It is, after all, every bit as relaxing and absorbing as gardening, or cooking, or flower arranging, and much less fleeting!

The fleece shown opposite was dyed from a 'roving' that is, a long, continuous pre-carded and scoured length of undyed fleece with all its fibres lying in the same direction. It is bought in this state from fleece suppliers and is ready to spin or dye.

For this sample, chemical dyes were used, (powder in small tins obtainable from hardware stores), and small batches of the fleece were dyed separately in different strong colours according to the manufacturer's instructions. After drying, the dyed batches were then split up and carded to mix the colours together. Spun fairly finely and then plyed, the effect is beautiful multi-coloured yarns similar to the ones seen in the photograph.

To create a lovely colourful yarn from start to finish and then to go on and make something with it is worth every bit of the time it takes. The looks of wonder and amazement on the faces of those who see us wearing these entirely hand-made creations defy description, and yet it is within the capability of anyone. Even those who do not possess a spinning wheel can easily learn to use a spindle; it only takes a little practice, patience and perseverance to make yarns as colourful as those shown here.

The photograph of the knitted and crocheted techniques shown on page 72 is a small detail from a rainbow cushion belonging to Valerie Campbell-Harding. Inserted into it, here and there, are small areas of canvas work, which can be seen just above the centre. This technique is explained on page 96 and opens up even more possibilities for the use of colour, pattern and texture.

A passing glance at the apricot-coloured roses shown on page 73 may be enough for many people, but to the artist and those with an interest in colour, there is much more to be seen than apricot. Look deeply into the flowers and see the shadows and subtle mixtures of tones. Note how the edges of the petals differ from the insides and how they each reflect a certain amount of colour from those next to them. Throughout this small sample the yarns have been changed very frequently, so that hardly two stitches together are the same.

Dyeing yarns at home

Natural-dyed yarns are typified by a softness of tone which is difficult to achieve by any other means. Gathering the plants and preparing them takes time and effort, but the results are unique and infinitely satisfying.

There is no shortage of good books on natural dyeing techniques, and if the idea appeals to you, obtain one from your local library and start from there.

Chemical dyes for experiments

If you prefer to use the chemical method, however, there are reliable dyes available to help you do this with great ease. On the understanding that any results you achieve will almost certainly be surprising, (even when you are sure that you know what you are doing), the time and effort taken to dye your own yarn, fleece or knitting can be well worthwhile and always fun. This is particularly so when trying to obtain a variation of colour, (or colours), within one hank, called 'random-dyeing' - and never was a name more apt!

Classroom dyeing for project work

Teachers find home, or classroom dyeing, particularly useful in obtaining unity of colour for a project, when all they have to begin with is a box full of assorted yarns and colours.

Any kind of yarn, except acrylic, can be dyed with powdered hot or cold-water dyes. The amount of dye absorbed by the yarn will depend on its composition, the strength of the dye, and the time you leave it in the dye-bath. It will also depend somewhat on the temperature of the water and whether or not you add salt to make absorbancy more effective and vinegar to fix the dye.

For assorted yarns of mysterious composition, first skein them into separate skeins and tie them into tidy units with the special figure-of-eight knot shown in the diagram, (see below). Do this at least four times for each skein to prevent tangling in the water and during drying. Now wet the skeins thoroughly in warm water.

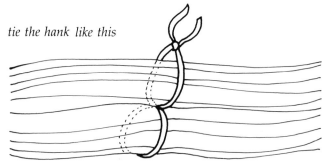

tie the hank like this

While the yarns are soaking, make up a tin of dye, by placing the powder in a jug and pouring boiling water *gently* over it, stirring to dissolve. At this stage

you should also add two or three tablespoons of common salt and about quarter of a pint of vinegar. Make this solution up to about one pint with cold or hot water. One tin of dye will do for about one pound weight of yarn.

Into a large old vessel, pour the dye solution and add enough water, (preferably warm), to cover the yarn completely - you will have to guess how much is needed at this stage. Now lower the wet yarn into the dye-bath and allow it to submerge completely.

The easiest method of achieving a good result is to leave the yarns in the dye overnight and rinse them out the following day. If this is not feasible, leave the yarns in the dye for at least half an hour, after which they should be lifted out at intervals to see what effect the dye is having. Note that when wet the colour will appear darker than it actually is, so allow for this when deciding when to remove the yarns. Natural fibres, (wool, cotton and linen), will accept dye very readily; others may take longer.

For non-functional uses, where the yarns are unlikely to be washed again, this method is perfectly adequate and fool-proof. However, I use both hot and cold-water dyes in this way with good results, even for garments, but you must choose whether to take the risk of not boiling. What you *will* get is a new batch of yarns with one over-colour and some unity which was not apparent previously. Remember though, that you cannot make dark colours lighter, and the original colour of the yarn will blend with that of the dye to make another third colour. These are the exciting bonuses of hand-dyeing.

The oven method

There are various methods of random-dyeing using pots and jars, but the one which I find easiest to use is the oven method, (see below), and I have tried it many times with great success.

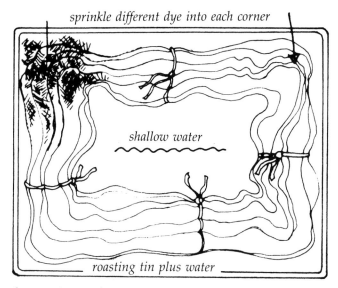

sprinkle different dye into each corner

shallow water

roasting tin plus water

do not stir or agitate
bake in oven at 350°F for about one hour

You need a large, deep roasting tin and three different coloured dyes, (try red, blue and yellow), plus some salt and vinegar. Skein the yarns and tie them as before, or use pieces of fleece, and wet them thoroughly in warm water. Half fill the roasting tin with water, then add two or three tablespoons of common salt and about quarter of a pint of vinegar. Lay the yarn in the water. Using the tip of an old knife, sprinkle a small amount of the dry dye on to the wet yarn in each corner of the tin, one colour in each corner. Be careful not to agitate or swish the water too much but allow the colours to merge unaided.

Place the tin carefully into the oven set at about 350°F for approximately one hour, then remove and leave to cool undisturbed. Rinse thoroughly.

Red, blue and yellow should merge to give the three secondary colours of orange, green and violet in various depths, so this will be a true rainbow yarn! To obtain more subdued pastel colours, use slightly diluted dye instead of the 'neat' powder.

Colour schemes

A splash of contrasting red amidst the mass of fern leaves directs the eye towards what is generally called the 'focal point', that is, the part of a design which attracts the eye towards it and invites closer investigation. This scheme has been simulated in this small detail of knitting and crochet. Contrasts can be seen in the light and dark tones.

Overleaf
The four small panels shown on page 76 are attempts to match yarns with the colours of the four seasons. Each one measures the size of a postcard and is a mixture of knitting and crochet. Only six or seven yarns have been used for each sample but they could be the basis for another project, perhaps a set of four cushions or larger wallhangings.

Once the technique of mixing free style knitting and crochet has been mastered, it will be appreciated how much more difficult it is to make a small piece of fabric than a large one. The desire to give a free rein to many colour tones and textures can be quite inhibited when working to a small scale, and it is only when one can wander about freely, taking as much room as one needs, that one learns how to exploit all the possibilities of stitch, yarn and technique to their fullest extent. However, for those who prefer small scale work, my advice is to seek out finer yarns and tools, and begin from there.

This photograph on page 77 shows a detail of a large piece of free style knit/crochet fabric which formed part of a coat. The different types of yarn can clearly be seen. No attempt is made to segregate natural yarns from synthetic: all are used together. Random dyed yarns are partly useful as are those which have flecks of different colours in them. Some stitches are laid over the top of others to soften the effect, and often two or three colours are used together to make the change from one to another more gradual.

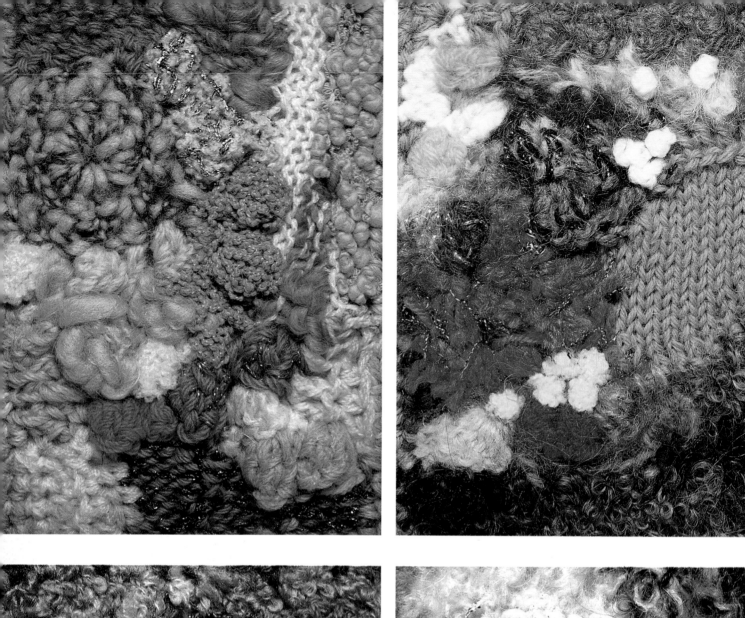
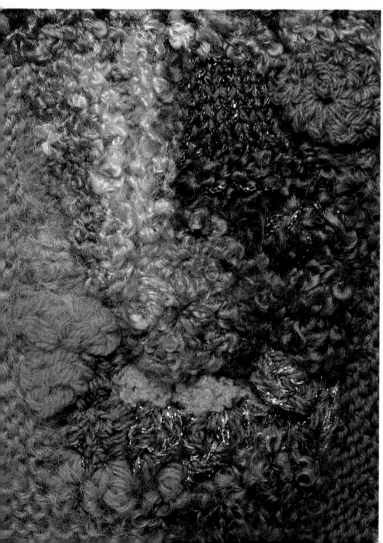
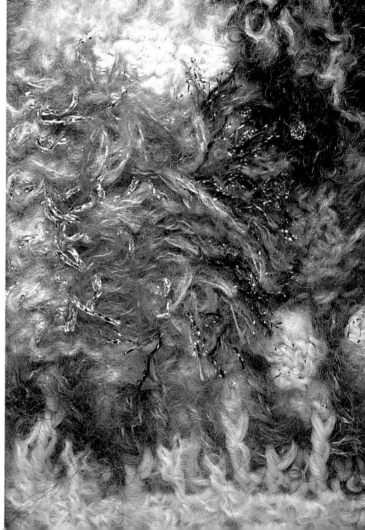

Experiments in moving colours

Crochet is all too often spoilt by unimaginative use of stitches and yarns which produce bland, all-over patterns or rigid lines of unbroken colour.

Sylvia Cosh overcomes these problems by discovering ways of making stitches 'break away from their moorings' and plunge down into previous rows, taking the yarn and colour with them.

Similarly, she exploits the varying heights of crochet stitches, (something which cannot be done in knitting), to make wavy rows. When these rows of long and short stitches are combined with changes of yarn and texture at random, the effect is of a more subtle nature than the mere repeat of a stitch in a set pattern. In addition to this, the yarns she uses are mostly 'broken' colours, so that the tiniest glimpses of colour

contrasts peep out here and there making the effect of even straightforward pattern rows more interesting and unique.

As crochet stitches are larger than knitted ones, two-colour patterns present more problems. Moreover, crochet stitches are not square, or even rectangular, so Jacquard crochet is not very easy to plan. However, this sample shows how multi-coloured crochet comes into its own when used in an abstract design, where the precise shapes of recognisable objects are not so critical.

Meandering, jigsaw shapes, like clouds, float along between straight lines, happily changing form and yarn, while the stitch remains constant. Consequently, hard and horizontal row lines are barely noticeable,

Seascape Designed and tapestry woven by **Beryl Tilley**

especially as the use of brushed yarns also helps to disguise this trait. As with embroidery, one has to experiment to discover the types of design suitable for the technique being used and not to assume, as many do, that all is possible to all methods.

Yarns used in the woven tapestry shown above were handspun on a drop spindle and a spinning wheel. It clearly illustrates the use of smooth and textured yarns in a style not unlike the Scottish Islands knitted panel shown on page 37.

The advantages of designing in this technique are several. Although the work progresses from the bottom, as knitting usually does, the rows can be left incomplete while the areas along the same level are built up independently. Another advantage is that the work is held rigidly in front of the worker who can see the effects of each move instead of having to wait until the fabric is pulled out and turned around, as the knitter does. It doesn't curl up, either!

Many different yarns can be used in the same area without the attendant problems of weaving-in or stranding. Yarns are wound on to card or wooden bobbins, (rather like pencils), and left to hang down. Tension is never the same problem to tapestry weavers as it is to knitters; one can make use of any yarn or thread in the same design, however thick or thin, textured or smooth.

'Seascape' shows how very subtle effects of colour are produced by using finer yarns of different colours and tones close together. Note particularly how the tones of blue change to give an impression of ripples and depth, and the mixture of fine reds and blues in the foreground produces a rich brown. This is a more interesting effect than would have been achieved by using brown yarn. The range of colours used in this design is actually quite limited and yet the effect is lively because of the way in which they have been blended. One distinct advantage which tapestry-weaving has over knitting is that there are no elongated stitches to interfere with the smooth horizontal and curved lines, no 'stepping', no broken lines; all is smooth.

The correct, (professional), method of working on a tapestry requires the weaver to work from the back of the fabric with the many yarn-holding bobbins hanging down before her so that they can easily be picked up again as needed. The drawn design, (the cartoon), is placed on the other side of the warp in an upright position so that the weaver can see it through the threads and follow its shapes.

No disadvantages? Ah! Well, yes; one or two! Vertical lines are a bit more of a problem, especially to a beginner, than they are to knitters. Some old tapestries actually have vertical slits where colours adjoin each

79

other though modern weavers often make use of this effect in a design. Another disadvantage, and probably the main one for me, is that tapestry-weaving is not so easily portable and will never fit into a handbag in quite the same way as knitting and crochet. But of course one could always try a miniature tapestry. What a lovely thought!

Above
A detail from the Seascape
Here one is able to see the mixture of reds and blues in the foreground, producing a rich brown when seen at a distance. Note also the mixture of blue tones and salmon red tones higher up; these mixtures create a subtlety of movement which flat colours could not achieve.

Wool 'n rings

This chapter solves the problem of how to mount and display
a superb example of knitting, or a combination of knitting and crochet.
Circular frames of wood, or wire, or lampshade frames,
make ideal supports to satisfy both functional and decorative needs.

Covering frames with knitting and crochet

Mounting knitted or crocheted fabric on rings for decorative purposes is an excellent way of displaying the structure of the stitches and textures, colours and yarns, while keeping the fabric in shape and, allowing the light to shine through, or complement the colour of a wall. The fabric to be mounted in this way need not be circular. It needs only to be the same size, (or slightly smaller), than the ring for which it is intended; it will stretch to fit the sides.

Metal rings can be bought at craft shops and on craft counters in many large stores. They are generally made of copper, though polished wooden ones are attractive. They are often slightly thicker than the metal ones. A range of sizes is usually available, from about 4ins/10cms to 22ins/56cms in diameter. The ones seen in the illustrations here and on the following pages are between 8ins/20.5cms and 10ins/25.5cms across, the garden circle on page 85 being the largest size available.

Lampshades can also be covered with knitting, crochet, or a mixture of the two, as explained in the section on 'Wool 'n texture'. The frame should be covered in the same way as for rings, so that the bare metal does not show where the lacy holes occur.

It is not *essential* to bind metal rings, though a chained or bound edge is useful for sewing on to if the centre pieces are to be made separately. The 'filling' can also be made *in situ* on the ring, taking the yarn across from one side to the other with the hook, slip-stitching it to the opposite side, then on to another part. This structure of yarn can then be worked on with chains, loops and masses of random stitches in a variety of textured yarns to make a very free-style and exciting design.

The ring seen below is quite a small one, and contains a mixture of knitting and crochet in both textured and smooth yarns. Lacy holes add to the attraction of the fabric, and these can be stretched quite taut to fit the ring at any point. The crochet edging can clearly be seen on this example, and the very odd-shaped piece of fabric was pulled to fit, first by pinning and then by sewing. The yarn used for the bound edge was the same colour as the main part, not a contrast, as it is usually better to allow the circle to blend in with the background. Little crocheted cups and domes and wooden beads have been added to the surface; these were all sewn on after the ring had been assembled.

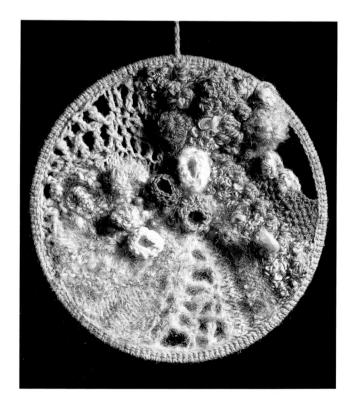

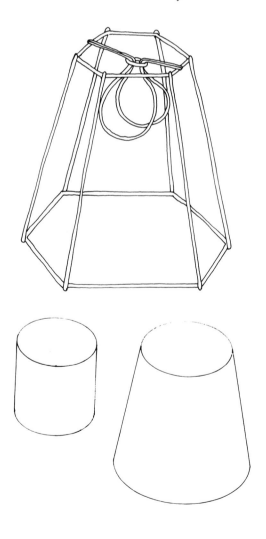

Binding a ring with crochet

1) Wedge the metal ring firmly against your body and hold the top of it in your LH. This will prevent it flapping about as you work.
2) Take the supply yarn in your LH, make a loop and hold the tail of it along the top of the ring.
3) Take the hook in your RH, pass it under the top of the ring, and pull the loop of yarn to the front and up to the top. Keep the supply yarn at the *back* of the ring.

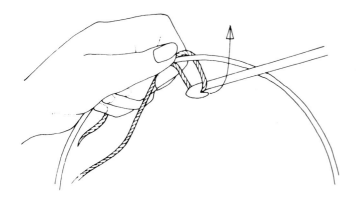

4) Yoh and pull through as in a dc - one stitch made. Keep the supply yarn in the LH and hold the top of the ring. Again pass the hook under the top of the ring, catch the supply yarn, pull up to the top, yoh and pull through the loop on the hook. Another stitch made.
5) As you proceed, work the stitches over the tail end, and continue to make dc sts all round the ring, keeping them even and regularly spaced.

   Note: a slightly different handling technique is necessary to be able to manoeuvre the hook under and over the rigid metal ring. Hold it in an *overhand* grasp, (as for a tennis racquet), and exaggerate the arm and shoulder movements to pick up the yarn and make the stitches.

6) As you reach the first stitch again, close the gap by working a ss into it, leaving a longish end of yarn before cutting it off.
7) Now the ring is covered, twist the chained edge towards the inside so that your knitted/crocheted pieces of fabric can be sewn on to it.

On this all-crochet experiment, the ring was first bound, then crochet chains were taken from one side to the other and worked into, building up a series of patches. Where the stitches adjoined the edges they were taken into the binding and, in some cases, actually began there.
This example shows how completely random stitches and different textured yarns can be used to build up a circle. ▷

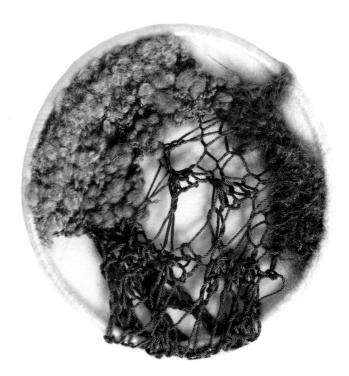

This simple experiment shows how any strange shape can be eased into a circle, even one that is wider than the diameter of the ring. In this case, the extra piece (top left), was taken over the ring to the back and stitched on to itself to create a double layer. This ring was bound by wrapping it with yarn around the edges.
The finer yarn was knitted on large needles and additional irregular holes were introduced by wrapping the yarn several times round the needle, (dropped stitches), and by simple decreasing and increasing on the same spot. △

Seasons' trees

Although you are seeing four separate photographs, the four trees are built on to two rings, back to back. They were made especially for the Knitting Craft Group in 1978 as a teaching aid and the idea has since proved immensely popular with people of all ages.

Through the lacy pink blossom of the spring version can be seen the green foliage of summer. The two trunks were made separately and fixed to the bottom of the ring. Chain 'branches' were then taken to the outer edges and worked upon, one layer for each side but then joined together later by 'filling-in' stitches. This can be seen more easily in the autumn/winter

ring, where the structure of the chained branches is left uncovered on one side.

Many yarns were used for each one, in different textures and tones of colour. One yarn alone will seldom express the variation of changes seen in the foliage of one tree. The technique used is the same as that described in the section on Wool 'n Texture, using knitting needles and crochet hooks with equal ease, working stitches at random and in all directions. Lacy holes are acceptable, even desirable, and no expertise is required.

This free-style knitted/crocheted hanging is based on a large wire ring, about 20ins/53cms in diameter. To begin, the large cluster of rocks in the centre was made in crochet, then other textures were added on to all sides, in all directions as previously described. Pale greens, greeny-greys, yellows and pale pinks were worked in here and there and as many highly-textured areas as possible were 'built in' by making crocheted bobbles in double yarns. Crochet loops, (chain fur st), also helped to suggest lush foliage.

The water, beginning its descent on the upper left hand side, started off as knitted stitches picked up from the edges closest to it, worked in rib in the direction of the water. This gradually widens and picks up other edges on the way and eventually, on larger and larger sized needles falls off the bottom to fray out into loose crochet and strands of yarn. The whole piece was made 'off the ring' but was then folded over the edges, (where the shape was not exact), and sewn on, slightly stretched.

It is always a good idea to bind the ring beforehand, even though you may cover it with the fabric, as this means that you can stitch into it where necessary, thus helping to stabilise the fabric. Once the fabric is fixed securely on to the ring by stitching, the whole of the back should be covered with very firm, heavy-duty interfacing. This should be cut only fractionally smaller than the finished piece so that no part of it shows from the front. It is then pinned on and sewn very neatly to the edge all the way round with matching sewing thread. If the weight of the knitting bulges forward in some places, it can then be caught back with a few stitches against the firm backing material. The hanging device can also be sewn on to this; I used two curtain rings placed on the edges of the ring near the top, with a cord strung between them.

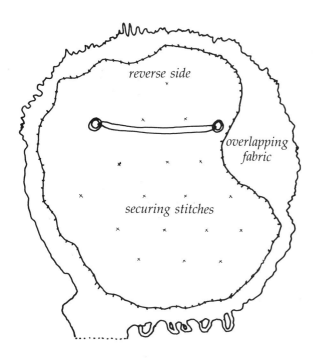

reverse side

overlapping fabric

securing stitches

Geode

This design is based on a geode, which is a phenomenon of the mineral world whereby a bubble of air is trapped inside cooling rock for millions of years, making a hole inside. When this is eventually discovered and sliced across, a crystal-covered cavity appears within the coloured mineral, often of great beauty.

A mixture of knitting, crochet and embroidery, (in this case, needleweaving), is based on two rings, the smaller one inside the larger. The background of hessian can be seen at the lower edge; on top of this are applied pieces of knitting and crochet in browns and deep golden-yellow yarns. Nestling among these pieces are crochet 'domes' in a variety of yellows and golds, and woven fabric has been frayed to create a rough texture here and there.

Bendable plastic-covered garden wire is bound with yarns and then bent into winding curves to emphasise the shape and to give unity to the design. This has the effect of leading the eye to encourage exploration of the nooks and crannies.

The smaller ring of needleweaving is placed slightly away from the background so that it casts a shadow on the smooth sequin-covered paper behind. The bronze and gold beads also help to reflect the light around the most interesting area. The completed piece is backed on to an old dartboard.

Mobiles

These simple ideas are great fun to make and will encourage children to experiment with colours and techniques.

Double ring

1) Bind both rings with yarn.
2) Take chains across *one* ring to act as structures upon which to build stitches.
3) Fix this ring inside the second one at right angles, as shown, and stitch together.
4) Take chains across second ring *through the chains of the first one*.
5) Work on both sets of chains to build up a free-style design of lacy holes and textures.
6) Hang up near a window as a mobile.

Knitted ribbons in a ring

A perfect way to display long narrow strips of knitting or crochet, (perhaps the first efforts of a group of children), inside a ring. Simply stretch them across from one side to the other, either straight, (as shown), or diagonally, fold the ends over the ring and sew down. Even crochet chains can form part of the design, and tassels or pom-pons will complete the effect.

Hanging figure

A very small ring forms the head of this knitted or crocheted figure; the features are formed by tiny curtain rings hanging from the top. The woollen fringe of hair is knotted into the ring, a wooden bar forms the 'shoulder hanger', and a simple piece of rectangular knitting or crochet forms the body. Use colourful tassels and beads for the arms and legs.

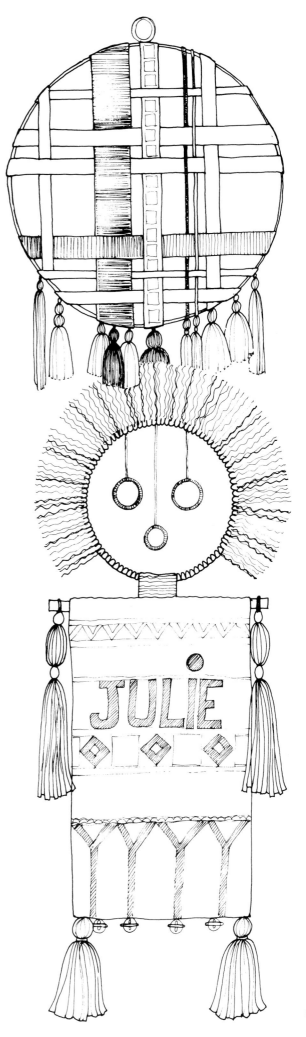

87

Lampshade in Shetland lace

Fishtail stitch has been used for this delicate lampshade.

Materials: one 25gm ball of white 3-ply yarn; one pair No 12/2¾mm needles; one pair No 14/2mm needles; one crochet hook for binding the frame; a blunt wool-needle for sewing-up.
One lampshade frame measuring 5ins/12.5cms high with six panels each measuring 3ins/8cms across the widest part and 1¾ins/4.5cms across the narrowest (top) part.

Tension: each knitted panel will appear to be considerably smaller than the frame panels, but this is necessary as the pieces are stretched on to the frame to enhance the lacy structure. The tension is 10 sts and 13 rows to 1in/2.5cms over stocking stitch on size No 14/2mm needles. The pattern is worked over 20 sts with the addition of two selvedge stitches at each side.

Lampshade panel: with size No 12/2¾mm needles, cast on 24 sts loosely. Knit 2 rows to begin. Commence pattern.
1st row k2, *yo, k3, sl 1, k2 tog, psso, k3, yo, k1*, rep from * to * to last 2 sts, k2.
2nd and every alternate row purl.
3rd row k2, *k1, yo, k2, sl 1, k2 tog, psso, k2, yo, k2*, rep from * to * to last 2 sts, k2.
5th row k2, *k2, yo, k1, sl 1, k2 tog, psso, k1, yo, k3*, rep from * to * to last 2 sts, k2.
7th row k2, *k3, yo, sl 1, k2 tog, psso, yo, k4*, rep from * to * to last 2 sts, k2.
8th row purl.
Work 3 complete patterns, (24 rows), then change to size No 14/2mm needles and work 2 more patterns (16 more rows).
Change to ss and work 15 rows, cast off purlwise on the 16th row.
Make five more pieces in the same way.

To complete: the lampshade frame should be bound with yarn before the knitted pieces are attached to it.
Pin the six panels together, (wrong sides facing), in a

continuous strip and then into a tube; sew them together with very tiny stitches, only taking in the extreme edges of each piece. When all six pieces have been stitched in this way, slip the tubular piece over the frame and pin the top edge in place with glass-headed pins pointing downwards against the tension. Use plenty of pins, then sew this edge to the binding on the frame using a neat over-and-over stitch, keeping the top very level and not allowing any of the binding to show on the front.

When this is complete, gently pull the lower edges of the knitting down to the base of the frame and pin in position with the pins pointing upwards. Make sure that the seams coincide with the upright struts of the frame, then sew this edge to the binding in the same way as before. Do not sew the knitting to the struts, only to the top and bottom edges.

Free-style lampshade

With lampshade making, one has the advantage that the fabric can be more lacy than would be practicable for garments. The light shining from the inside, lighting up the irregular holes, looks very effective, and in daylight the textures have a different appeal. An all-white or cream colour scheme is very attractive, especially with the addition of glitter threads, and for this type of project, where the fabric will not be under stress, the use of woven fabric strips of knitting and crochet comes into its own.

For this project, a paper pattern, (a template), can be made to the shape of the lampshade by rolling it along a piece of brown paper and drawing the edges as you go along. Cut this out and mould it round the frame to correct the shape and trim the edges. This is the shape of the lampshade and the fabric making can begin at any point. However, I have always found it more convenient to attach my growing fabric to the wire frame as soon as possible, and use the frame as a kind of 3-D template.

No lining is necessary, but the frame should be completely wrapped with yarn before you begin to attach the fabric to it. To sit with the frame on your knee, (or a table), whilst the incomplete work is attached to it is not as uncomfortable as it sounds and allows you to constantly check that you are doing the right thing in the right place.

When the fabric is big enough to reach right round and meet itself, the two parts can be sewn together invisibly and the rest of the space filled in, sewing and 'welding' as you go. There will be no straight joins anywhere, and these should all be quite invisible. The area of fabric needed for a lampshade is quite small. Stitch the top and bottom edges to the wrapping on the frame, using the same yarn, and keep the fabric under slight tension.

Laundering is no problem; simply immerse the complete frame in warm soapy water and leave it to soak, then gently swish to remove any dust. Rinse gently in clear water and roll the lampshade on to a towel to remove excess moisture. Hang or stand to dry thoroughly, making sure that the wrapped frame is quite dry to prevent rusting.

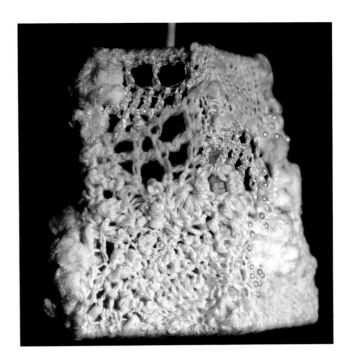

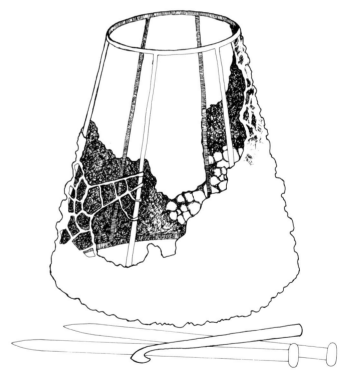

Dorset buttons

These handmade buttons are very similar in appearance to those used on the long strip coat seen on page 123. Those were based on plastic frames, but *these* are a type which have been made in the traditional manner for a long time and became the basis of a local industry among the people of Dorset. There are many different patterns, but all were based on rings of metal or bone of various sizes and were often used as fastenings on smocks. We used plastic curtain rings for our version, these being more readily available and safe to wash.

As it is very difficult to join threads once the process is under way, be sure to begin with a very long thread of yarn of at least 2¾yds/2½mtrs for a button of about 1in/2.5cms diameter. After making a trial button, you will be able to see more exactly how much you need.

Use a blunt tapestry needle with a large eye, and a pointed one for finishing off. Keep the stitches close together and begin by working buttonhole stitch all round the ring, working over the loose end with the first few stitches. When the last stitch has been joined firmly to the first one, turn the loops towards the inside as shown.

Now make a number of spokes by laying the thread across and round the bound ring, then hold these firmly in the centre with a tight cross stitch. Do not cut the thread, but begin to make firm back stitches round the threads as seen in the lower LH drawing, and continue until the centre is filled, (lower RH drawing). Make a few stitches at the back in the centre, and leave the extra thread hanging to sew to the garment.

The complete set may be made in the background colour of the garment, or you may prefer to draw more attention to them by picking up the colours used for the pattern in each one, as I have done. This makes them a decorative feature of the garment, not simply a fastening device.

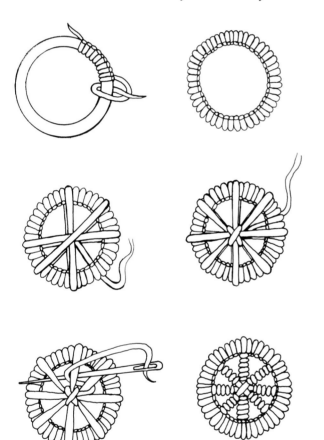

90

Wool 'n embroidery

Many embroiderers are already aware of the close affinity
between various textile techniques,
such as weaving, macramé, lace-making, knitting,
crochet, tatting and other less familiar skills.
It will therefore be no surprise to them to see well-known
embroidery techniques used in conjunction with
knitting and crochet, both formally and free-style.

Combining knitting and crochet with embroidery

To those people who know knitting and crochet only in the conventional sense, the combining of embroidery techniques with these crafts may come as quite a surprise. A look at knitted and crochet fashion today, however, will remind them that things are not what they used to be, and the innovative treatment of these fabrics has moved a long way in recent years.

So, for the embroiderer who is looking for new ways of extending her horizons towards even more decorative effects, and the fashion-orientated knitter or crocheter, ideas suggested in this chapter may spark off thoughts of wonderful experiments in these areas. It goes without saying that there are some embroidery techniques which lend themselves more easily than others to an integration with knitting and crochet; some even pretend to *be* each other!

Canvas embroidery provides one of the most comfortable associations with knitting and crochet, and the reader may like to practice a few of the simpler stitches ready for the big connection! Use either single or double canvas, whichever you prefer. The mesh size should, for practice, be anything between eight and twelve holes to the inch/2.5cms. Use ordinary *smooth* knitting yarns of a thickness which will pass through the holes easily, and a *blunt* tapestry or wool needle with a large eye. This should also be the correct size for the wool and for the holes of the canvas.

To begin, cut a piece of canvas measuring about 6ins/15cms square, just big enough to hold comfortably in your hand. To stop the wool catching on the prickly edges, bind the piece with masking-tape, or something similar. To work the first stitch, make a knot in the end of the yarn. Insert the needle into the canvas and leave the knot on the *right side* while you begin to make the stitch about 6 or 8 threads away from the knot. Work the stitches towards the knot, covering the strand across the back as you stitch, and when you reach the knot, cut it off. You should now have worked in the end of the yarn. After this, to begin each new yarn, run the end through the stitches which have already been made, but do this *on the wrong side* without tying a knot first.

Canvas work

These familiar embroidery stitches are all simple to work but form completely different textures.

Tent stitch worked over one vertical thread and one horizontal thread. It is used here to divide all the sections with a white line. It is the smallest canvas work stitch and is useful for filling in tiny gaps.

Chequer stitch uses nine tent stitches in a square alternately with a diagonal square stitch. This may be worked in one or two colour threads.

Cross stitch (no diagram) the first two rows show the top threads lying in the same direction and the next two rows show the top thread lying in alternate directions.

Upright and diagonal crosses worked in two colours. The upright cross worked over two threads is made between each diagonal cross over two threads.

Cushion stitch is like chequer stitch without the tent stitch squares. The diagonal squares can be worked in the same direction or in the opposite direction, (as shown here), in one colour or two.

Scottish stitch is another mixture of a diagonal square and tent stitch. This may be worked in one or more colours.

Straight stitch (no diagram) worked over 2, 3 or 4 threads, makes interesting patterns in one or more colours.

Upright Gobelin stitch (no diagram) a simple straight stitch which may be worked over 2 or more threads.

Satin stitch is a sloping straight stitch which should not be worked over too many threads as these may catch. Not a good covering stitch.

Brick stitch is useful for shading several tones of the same colour. Here, two blues and white are used.

Florentine stitch (not shown on sample) is more of a pattern than a stitch; worked over various numbers of stitches in an upright formation using different colours to create a large variety of formal patterns.

Rice stitch is made in two parts, a large diagonal cross over four threads with a smaller stitch going across each corner. In the sample, the centre row makes use of two colours.

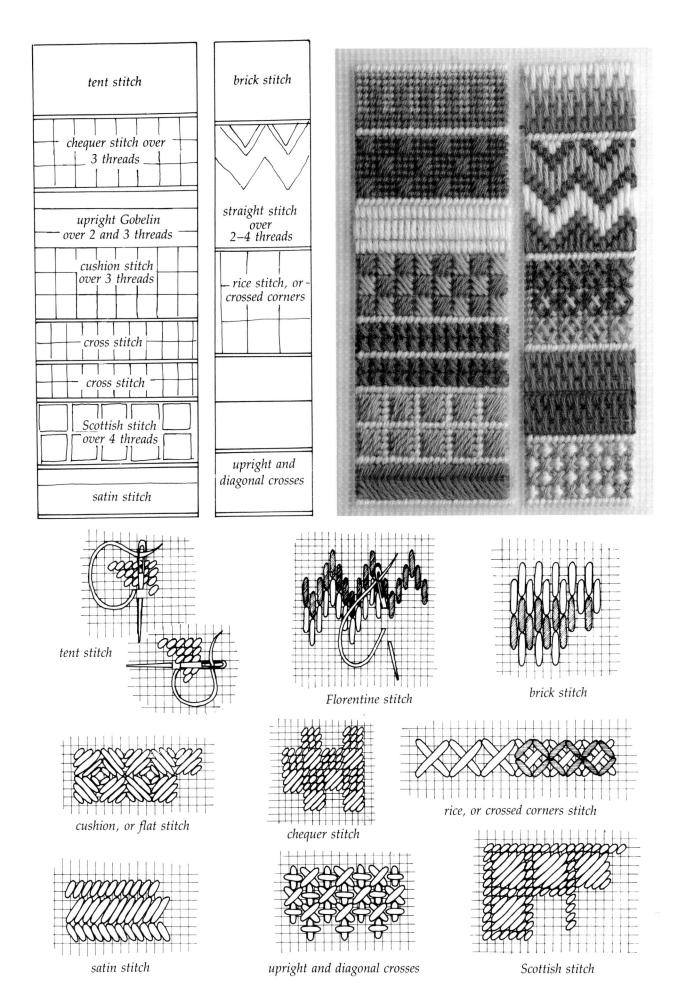

tent stitch

brick stitch

chequer stitch over 3 threads

straight stitch over 2–4 threads

upright Gobelin over 2 and 3 threads

rice stitch, or crossed corners

cushion stitch over 3 threads

cross stitch

cross stitch

Scottish stitch over 4 threads

upright and diagonal crosses

satin stitch

tent stitch

Florentine stitch

brick stitch

cushion, or flat stitch

chequer stitch

rice, or crossed corners stitch

satin stitch

upright and diagonal crosses

Scottish stitch

93

A selection of yarns dyed with plant dyes by Wendy Tomlin from the plants gathered around her home in Scotland was used by the author to design this small canvas embroidery. For those who have access to a selection of plants from garden and/or countryside, almost everything will produce some kind of colour, though most need a mordant to bring out the best ones. Easily available to many of us in the country or within reach of wild land are such plants as parsley, (cow- *and* the edible variety), elderberry, blackberry, privet, mint, ivy, dahlia and onion-skins. The colours produced have a unique softness of tone all of which appear to blend in harmony. Placed with plenty of white, they can hardly go wrong.

The stitches used here are all conventional ones with more than a hint of Florentine. This breaks out of its usual composure into a more random flowing design punctuated by cushion stitch, which is the squared one with stitches lying in opposite directions to each other. The design is abstract, made by simply following the inclination of the stitches, tones and lines in relation to each other. Avoid trying always to 'see pictures' in things, but rather try to appreciate a design from the point of view of its colours, shapes and textures alone.

This sample was worked on plastic canvas and would make a very attractive cover for a notebook or one side of a purse.

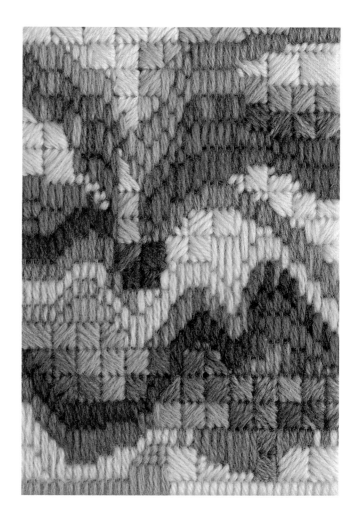

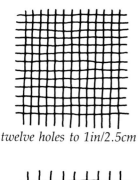
twelve holes to 1in/2.5cm

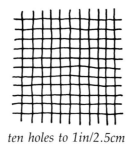
ten holes to 1in/2.5cm

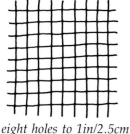
eight holes to 1in/2.5cm

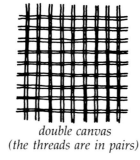
double canvas (the threads are in pairs)

Sizes of canvas are established by the number of holes to the inch or 2.5 cms. This is known as the mesh size. The size of the mesh you choose will depend on your eyesight and the type of yarn you wish to use, but to begin you will probably find that ten or twelve holes will be most useful, especially for 3/4-ply yarn or DK thickness.

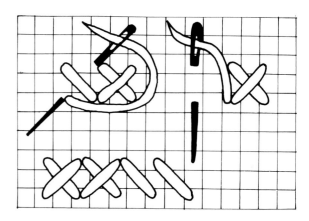

Cross stitch: one of the simplest canvas work stitches, usually made over two threads of the canvas, both vertically and horizontally. The top thread should lie in the same direction on each stitch, whether to the left or right. It is not important whether the first layer is worked all at once or whether each stitch is completed individually, but when the crosses are to be integrated with knitted/crocheted fabric, the latter method is preferable.

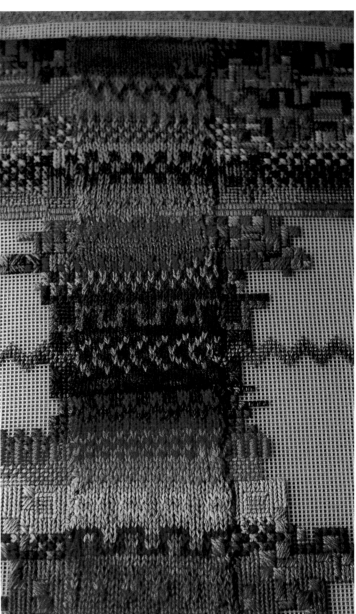

A canvas work and knitting experiment.

The similarity between formal multi-colour knitting, (commonly called Jacquard knitting), and canvas work patterns prompted me to try out an experiment to see how the two could be fused together. A long piece of knitting was made in stocking stitch and covered with simple, two-colour patterns each of very few rows. The piece measures about 15 × 5ins/38 × 13cms, and used double-knitting yarns on No 10/3¼mm needles.

The knitting was pressed, and laid on to a piece of single plastic canvas, (14 holes to 1in/2.5cms), and tacked firmly in position all the way round. Using exactly the same yarns, canvas work stitches were extended from the side edges encroaching on to the knitting to make the transition as invisible as possible. The two illustrations above show the various stages of development. In the process, all kinds of things were discovered about the similarity in techniques, for instance, between stocking stitch (knitting) and knitting stitch (canvas work), and how the same patterns change in translation from one technique to the other.

To make full use of the differences in behaviour, (as well as the similarities), of the two techniques is another angle which could be explored. The knitting should be allowed to make shapes which would be difficult or impossible in canvas work, and the latter should retain the crisp rigidity inherent in its composition. On looking at them together, however, a unity will be seen to exist which would cause the observer to wonder, at first, which was which.

Free-style knitting and crochet with canvas work

We have already seen an example of the way knitting can be combined with canvas work in a formal way, matching the patterns and transferring them from one to the other. The design, shown opposite, combines it in a more free-style way with the knitted and crocheted combination fabric explained in the section on Wool 'n texture by making 'purpose-built holes'. To fill this, use a piece of embroidery canvas with a medium-sized mesh such as 10–12 holes to 1in/2.5cms, through which the same yarns will pass as those used *on the edges of the hole*. From the canvas, cut a shape which will completely cover the hole as shown in the diagram, below, then stitch it firmly in place with contrasting cotton. These stitches are removed when the embroidery is complete. Canvaswork stitches can now be worked directly on to this 'patch'.

An important point to remember when preparing this 'purpose-built hole' is that only *smooth threads and yarns* can be used comfortably on canvas, not textured ones. This means that all the yarns used on the edges of the hole must be of the kind which can also be used to make stitches on canvas because it is these same yarns which will be making the first stitches from the edges. These edge stitches are worked into *both* the knitted and crocheted fabric and the canvas at the same time to cover up any tiny gaps which may show and also to secure the two fabrics together.

The concept behind this method is the difference in level, stitch pattern and amount of detail possible. The colours should be the same as those used on the knitted and crocheted fabric and should therefore blend in just the same way as they do when used in the fabric, not contrast. The size and shape of the inset depends on factors such as the purpose, scale of the complete piece, and practical feasability but, in theory, any shape or size can be used. The patch shown here is about 3ins/8cms at its widest point.

The edge of the canvas can be trimmed back after completion, or, if used on a wall hanging, left in place. If there is a risk of fraying, the edges can be oversewn, but better still is the use of plastic canvas. However, if this method is to be used on garments, the practicalities of insets, and the placing, will have to be thought out.

The worked examples show how stitches are used at random to move the colours from the edges of the hole towards those colours on the opposite side. The fun

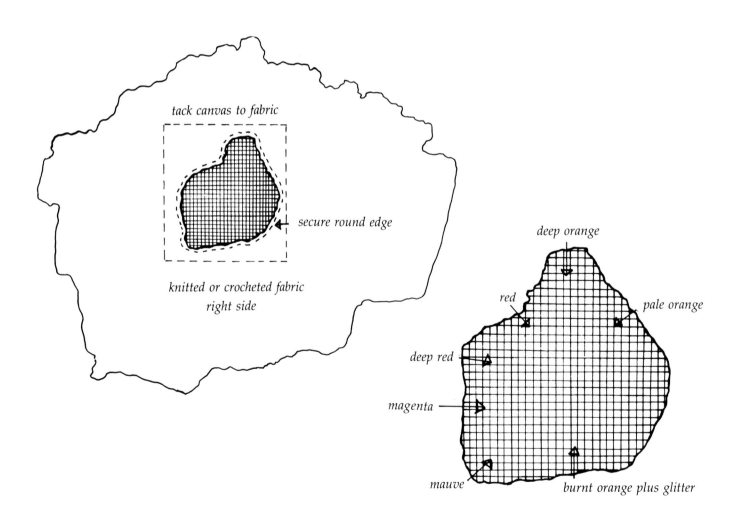

tack canvas to fabric

secure round edge

knitted or crocheted fabric
right side

deep orange

red

pale orange

deep red

magenta

mauve

burnt orange plus glitter

96

begins when it is obvious that a colour-change must take place, (say from pale orange to magenta), in a space of about 2ins/5cms. It can be done in various ways:

a) by using double yarn, (i.e. two different colours), and changing one of them at a time.

b) by overlaying stitches of one colour with a finer thread of another, gradually changing it altogether.

c) 'spotting' stitches of different colours together (i.e. same stitch, different colours or tones).

d) using a wide variety of different toned yarns to grade the colours gently.

Note: it is safer to begin by moving from *all edges* simultaneously towards the centre, so that no particular area begins to dominate before the others are established.

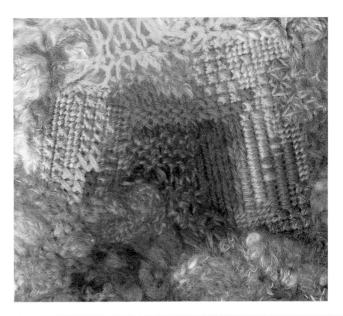

Canvas work stitches that resemble knitting

These diagrams show canvas work stitches which are particularly useful because of their resemblance to knitting and which can therefore be used to extend a colour on to the canvas in a way which is only noticeable by the change of level.

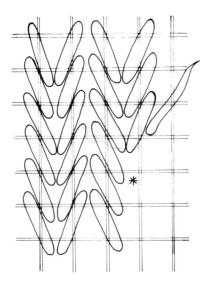

Knitting stitch, perfectly named and hardly distinguishable from the real thing except at close quarters. It can also be worked diagonally and can be made longer if need be.

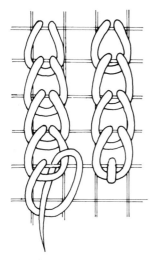

Chain stitch is more generally known as a free-style stitch but can be worked equally well on canvas with a very close resemblance to knitting.

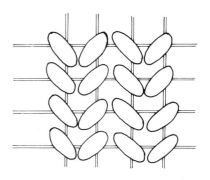

Reverse tent stitch worked in opposite directions looks like fine knitting.

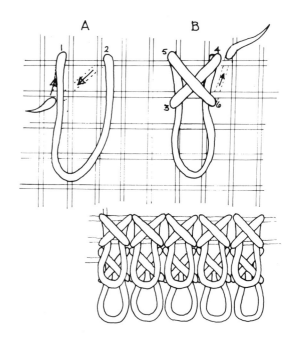

Astrakhan, or velvet stitch, is a loop stitch which resembles its knitted and crocheted counterparts and as with these, the loops can be snipped open and sheared to look like close pile. There is another simpler version of a pile stitch known as Turkey stitch.

Note: always work this stitch from the bottom upwards.

Rainbow sample

This richly textured piece of knitting and crochet contains a small patch of canvas work. The formal arrangement of the stitches, the lower level of the canvas and the finer detail are the main differences, though these can only be spotted at closer investigation. From a distance, the colours blend. Stitches are taken into both the knitting and the canvas around the edges so they are firmly secured together.

The black-and-white example shown here illustrates a way in which a practice piece might be tried without involving colour, just to get the idea of the method. The same yarns are used in the knitting and the embroidery to give continuity. In some cases, the stitches resemble knitting very closely.

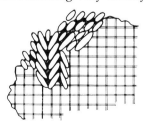

Openwork textures

One of the many advantages of using knitting and crochet in embroidery is the versatility of the fabric, its manipulative qualities and the way in which it can be made as dense or as open as needed for whatever purpose.

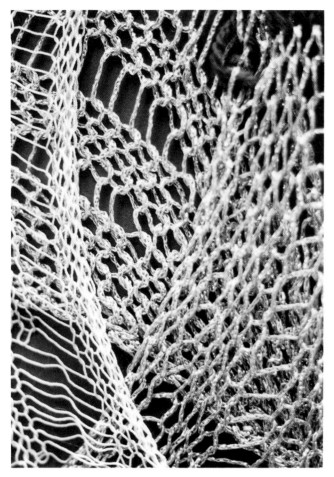

This sample shows very loosely knitted silver thread with stitches dropped to make ladders, pulled tightly to open up the mesh and fixed into a curve, worked by James Walters on a knitting machine. More open knitting, with ladders, is laid over this to create a double layer of holes. Three-dimensional structures and large panels can be made using this idea, as the openwork knitted fabric curves of its own accord when under tension. △

This sample shows long stitches in knitting, made by wrapping the yarn more than once around the needle, working only once into it on the next row and dropping the rest of the loop. The holes produced can then be worked on with traditional pulled-work stitches. On the edges of the holes, a row of hemstitch has been worked, with a simple twisted stitch in the centre. The centre panel has here been woven into with lengths of knitting ribbon. △

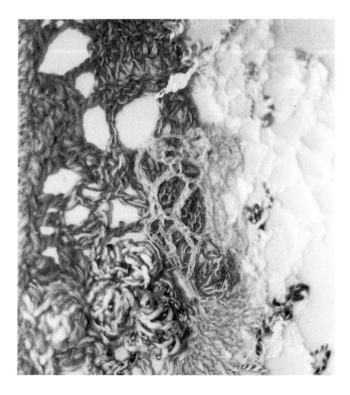

This sample shows loose and irregular crochet in a wide variety of threads and yarns (all grey and white) was used to create this openwork texture which resembles rocks, soil and loose pebbles. Random-dyed yarns containing tiny flecks of other colours add even more interest, though care must be taken not to allow these flecks to assume a regular pattern. ▷

Tree and Sunset
*Designed and embroidered by **Sue Pullinger**.*

Quilting and padding

The possibilities for quilting and padding the stretchy fabrics of knitting and crochet are one of its main attractions to embroiderers. Even the densest fabric has a certain amount of elasticity and most are so well-behaved and co-operative that there is little one cannot do with them in this area, particularly as there is no problem with frayed edges, as with woven fabrics.

Straight-sided patchwork pieces can be made by the following methods:
a) made separately of different yarns/colours, then sewn together.
b) made all in one piece in different colours, and quilted in the same way.

In fact, there is little to choose between these two methods for ease of working, as both have advantages and disadvantages. The small sample shown above, was made by the first method and has been further embellished, after quilting, by chain stitch and couching.

The detail of a stone wall sewn on to a background of 'free-style canvas work' is shown below. Each boulder was knitted separately, using ordinary double knitting and 3-ply yarns in a variety of simple stitches.

No particular shape was aimed for, as this depends more upon the shape of the card mount than on the knitting. Each knitted shape was backed by a small piece of thick card, padding was placed between this and the knitting to give a rounded shape, and the edges were then gathered and laced across the back.

The pieces are then arranged and stuck down into place, and stitches taken through the edges into the background for extra security. Some stones have been given an extra covering of green 'moss', worked in finer threads and fine needles, while others have orange lichen growing over them.

102

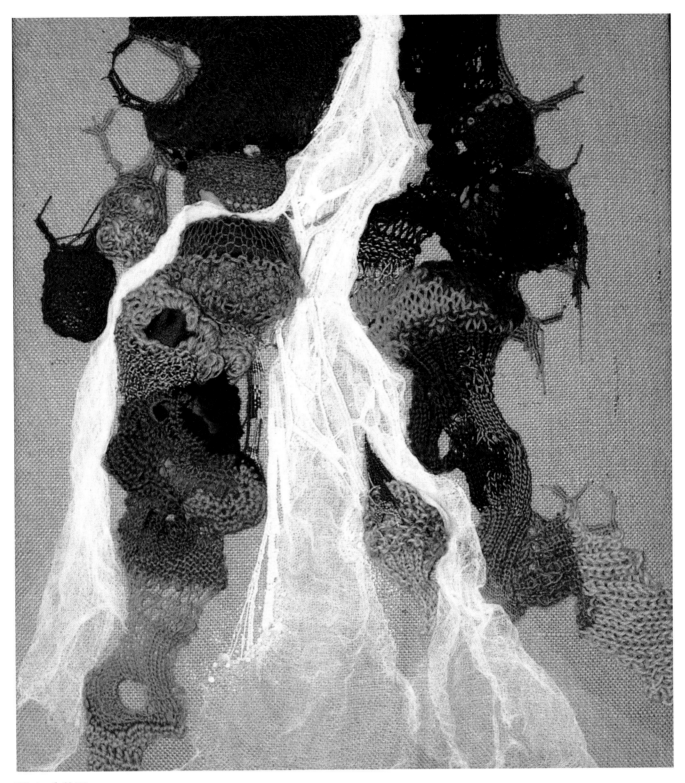

Waterfall II
This large panel is based on waterfalls remembered from a childhood in North Yorkshire, which became one of a series called 'My own North Country'.
The mossy boulders are made in a free-style mixture of knitting and crochet and are padded and highly textured. Between them run falls of water made from medical gauze and needle weaving.
This example shows how padding can be used in a dramatic way to create the effect of glimpses of scenery.

Designed and embroidered by **Freda Stoneman**

Gathered textures

Gathered effects and ruching in knitting, crochet and embroidery can all add texture to fabric.

At first glance, the photographs shown above may appear to be one and the same but look more closely and you will see the dividing line between the two, illustrating how the textures of knitting and embroidery can so closely resemble those in nature.

The piece on the left is part of an embroidery in which the designer has made use of long twisted pieces of reversed stocking stitch sewn to a background fabric and combined with crusty eyelet holes, wrapped threads, couched threads and French knots; the piece on the right is tree bark. Look at the photographs from a short distance away and the two will merge completely again.

The machine-knitted sample, right, in a combination of thick knitting yarns and crochet cotton was gathered into folds by thick furry wire, (bought from craft shops), woven in and out of the fabric. This not only adds extra colour but also helps to hold the folds in place.

Diagram of Seashore panel

This diagram shows the areas of knitting, crochet and canvas work.

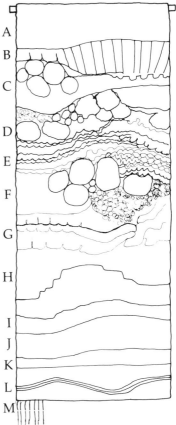

A. Dark brown knitting in thick yarn.

B. Irregular ribbing in plain and textured yarns.

C. Padded rocks applied to smooth knitting.

D. Crochet bumps in textured yarns.

E. Loosely knitted garter stitch.

F. Padded rocks applied to smooth knitting and crocheted textured yarn.

G. Distorted garter stitch.

H. Canvas work cross stitch on rug canvas base.

I. Knitting.

J. Ribbed and moss stitches.

K. Crochet.

L. Crochet lines worked over top of K.

M. Long fringe tied into edge.

Seashore

A long, narrow panel made of knitting and crochet with small areas of canvas work, mounted on rug canvas. The background of rug canvas not only keeps the fabric in shape but allows one to fill in areas between the various knitted pieces with canvas work stitches, attaching the fabric to the background at the same time. At the top, you can see how the knitted fabric has been gathered into folds.

This experiment can be used as a preliminary to a larger piece of work, allowing one to discover how the fabric behaves and how best to incorporate it into a design.

Smocking

Smocking is a favourite technique used on knitting, as the rib patterns make this easy, and can be varied to create different effects.

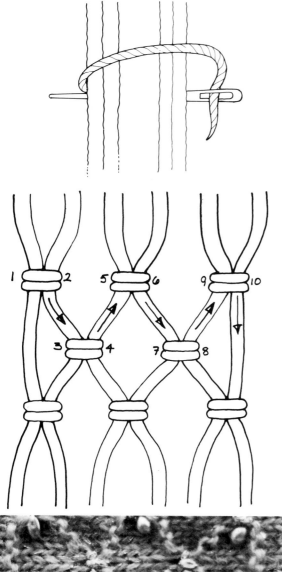

The example, above, shows a simple smocking stitch in metallic thread on a background of ribbing. Pieces of metallic/gold fabric have been applied to the spaces formed, and beads and sequins add extra sparkle. The effect is rich and would make a splendid patterned background to an embroidered panel, looking equally well on an evening bag. △

This sample shows ridges of reversed stocking stitch on a smooth background pulled together with embroidery. In this case, a metallic thread was used, and drop pearls were added, in the same colour as the knitting. The result is a very pretty textured panel which would look good on the fronts of an evening jacket or round the neck and cuffs.◁

The sample, below, shows straightforward ribbing, changing colours here and there, with pleats stitched across the ribbing which is then pulled into 'waves' and stitched in position. Beads accentuate the points. This can be done equally well on a plain background, on the right or reverse sides.▽

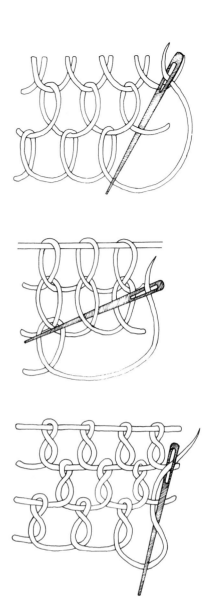

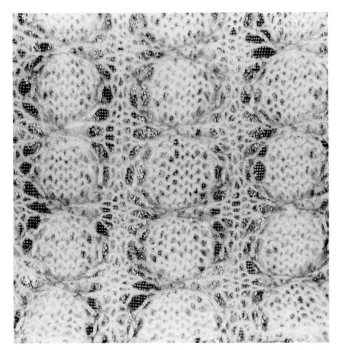

The sample of 'pulled fabric', above, is an embroidery technique which lends itself particularly well to knitting and crochet as this is so elastic and actually enjoys being pulled about. This small sample shows how a vertical pattern of ridges has been pulled out of shape with a delicate contrasting thread, creating an effect which could be used on the panel of a garment.△

Stitches like those shown here can be used to make an extra layer of lace-like threads over the top of knitting or crochet. These also help to hold knitting, (or crochet), in place on a background.

From the top, they are buttonhole filling stitch; centre, Ceylon stitch, which looks extraordinarily like knitting when worked closely and, at the bottom, a basic lace filling stitch of which there are other more complicated versions.

Canvas work and knitting

We have already seen how knitting, crochet and canvas work can be combined using the same yarns to move inwards from highly textured areas to a patch of smoother texture in the centre. This small sample shows how the opposite effect can be achieved. A piece of free-style knitted/crocheted fabric was made in an irregular shape, using a variety of knitting and embroidery threads. This piece was then tacked down on to a piece of canvas, (seen in the background), and the colours were extended from the edges into the canvas area, allowing them to fuse into each other. Stitches were chosen to disguise the edges of the fabric and blend them together with the canvas work. The colours also overlap on to the edges so that no hard lines appear. In some places this is so successful that it is difficult to tell where the fabric ends and the stitchery begins.

Whereas in the reverse method the fabric is pre-dominant and the canvas work of secondary importance, this is the other way round and the knitted/crocheted fabric becomes a highly textured island in a sea of canvas work.

Normally, in this embroidery technique, one cannot make use of very rough or bumpy yarns, nor can one take advantage of those which are too thick to go through the holes without resorting to applique; here they can all be used as long as some fine and smooth yarns are kept for the canvas work. This is a most rewarding combination of techniques, translating perfectly into colour/texture subjects rather than pictures.

This small sample is worked on 18 holes to 1in/2.5cms canvas, and makes use of textured knitting yarns, metallic threads, random-dyed silks, 3-ply Shetland yarns, crewel wools as well as stranded cottons.

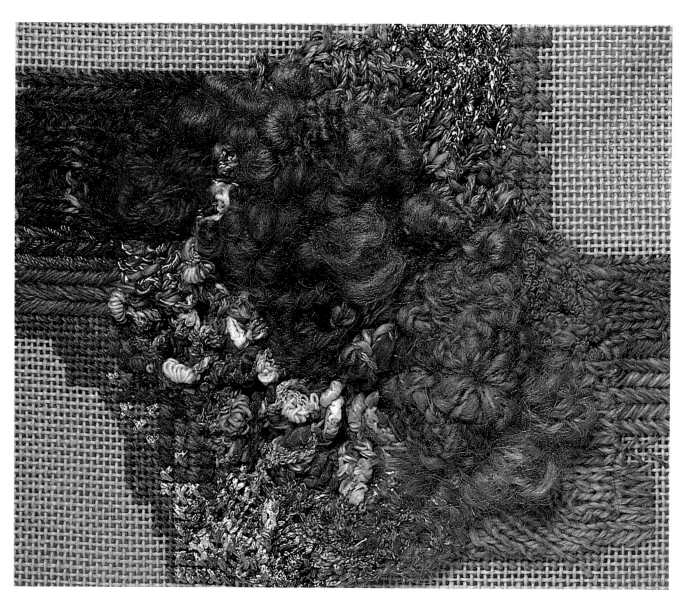

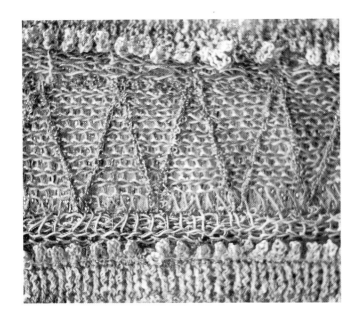

Machining with knitting

The sewing machine and knitted/crocheted fabrics go very well together, either with the machine foot on or off, straight stitch or zig-zag, or free-style. Try some samples along these lines to begin, and then experiment.

Strips of part-unravelled machine-knitting, top left, in a variegated rayon were machined on to a layer of sparkling fabric, and between these a layer of fine gold thread and cotton, (used together), has been stretched. Over this, lines of loose machine stitches have been worked, resulting in a pretty, delicate and sparkling effect suitable as a fashion detail on an evening garment.

Bottom left shows an experiment combining burnt holes in knitting with machine embroidery. Ordinary white yarn was burnt in several places and the result was laid over a piece of richly-patterned fabric. Tiny pieces of gold net were placed here and there, and spaces covered with stitchery over these. The resulting variations in pattern of the knitting and the fabric are interesting. The two layers of fabric are also bonded together very securely by this method, making a double fabric of great potential.

Machine stitchery over knitting on canvas below, shows very simple lines of zig-zag stitch in different widths, worked between the knit stitches of a random-dyed cotton yarn. All this set over the top of a scintillating and highly-reflective sheen fabric which shows through the tiny holes of the canvas and knitting. A firm and stiff fabric results, not good for wearables but excellent for embroiderers. Beads and sequins could also be added!

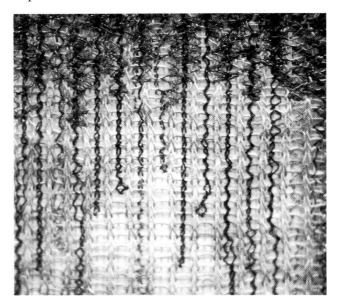

A small design embroidered by the author, using yarns spindle-spun and dyed by Patricia Baines.
The yarns are fine two-ply, chemically dyed, mostly couched on to the surface of coarse fabric, with some French knots, wooden and bone beads. The white areas show the natural white of the Romney marsh breed of sheep.

Couching

Some yarns, being fine and delicate, will not stand the constant pulling through fabric which embroidery stitches demand, and so the answer is to couch them down on to the surface of the fabric using sewing threads, silks or embroidery threads. Besides being an effective and pleasant method of working, it is also very economical as none of the top yarn appears on the underside, only the holding thread. There are several methods, but the one shown here is the simplest.

To begin to couch, the yarn must come up to the surface from below. The beginning of the yarn is taken through to the underside with a large needle, and fastened there with a few stitches, using the finer 'holding' thread.

To make the couched lines, use single or double thickness yarn, (double thickness has been used on this example), and lay the yarn on the surface. Bring the fine couching thread up to the surface near to the beginning as shown and take small neat stitches over the top of the yarn, keeping the beginning and end of each stitch slightly tucked underneath. Stitches should be unobtrusive in this method and should be made straight across the yarn, not at an angle.

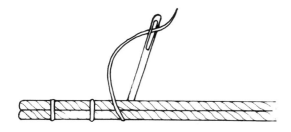

Keep the loose end of the yarn in place with pins, and move them along as you go. Small crosses can be used in the parts where the couched yarns cross each other, keeping both parts firmly in place.

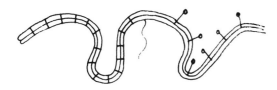

Work in any direction and keep the stitches, as far as possible, in neat rows as shown. Each stitch should be made in two movements, one coming up and one going down to avoid disturbing the thread lying on the surface.

Detail from the embroidery opposite.

Weaving with knitting and crochet

The reasons for using strips of knitting or crochet as weft and warp threads should be well considered before accepting the concept as another good idea, for it unfortunately has its uneconomical side. Weave strips of anything together, and at once half of them are covered up; do this with knitting or crochet strips and half of your efforts have disappeared from view! What you get is a fabric of double thickness, different on both sides and reversible.

If the fabric is to be designed specifically for a garment, then this characteristic may be acceptable and even desirable, but for a one-sided decorative fabric, such as for cushion covers or hangings, you may feel that similar effects could be created in a more economical way, by patchwork or quilted squares, perhaps.

There are other uses to which knitting and crochet can be put in connection with weaving, one of them being as a base into which other fabrics can be set.

The diagram below shows how simple filet crochet can be threaded with cut fabrics, crochet chains, ribbons, French knitting, lace edgings, cords and braids, cut plastic and soft leather. The resulting fabric can be used to make unshaped garments, bed rugs, cushion covers and bags.▽

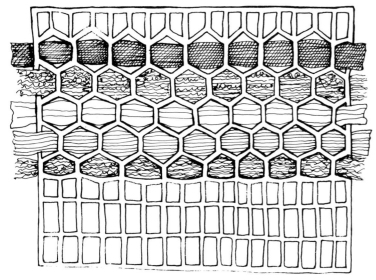

A small sample of cream-coloured filet crochet, above, has been threaded with sparkling yarns and narrow strips of pale pastel coloured fabrics.△

The sample, above, shows lengths of French knitting threaded through double rib. As the yarn used for both the background and cord was the same subtle random-dyed Shetland yarn, the colour/pattern/texture effect is very pleasing, and would make an extremely beautiful and firm fabric for a coat or jacket.
△

Wool 'n wearables

The most exciting and imaginative aspect of the alliance
of free-style knitting, crochet and embroidery is in garment design.
The previous chapters have been leading you gently to this
point and once you have taken your first magical step,
you will never again want to rely on published patterns.

Elements of design

There are as many ways of designing knitted and crocheted garments as there are designers. It seems that everyone tackles the process from a slightly different angle, (and for a different reason), to arrive at an end product which is a unique reflection of the personality behind it. Interest in the various aspects of garment design, such as the structure, shape, colour, texture, mathematics, economy, ease of making, will also be reflected through the designer into the garment, and this is just as well, as we must all be aware of these design elements to some extent.

If we are to begin to design our own knitted/crocheted garments, however, we must be aware of the main influences which are likely to affect our decisions, so that our plans are well thought out and leave nothing to chance that should have been taken into account at the beginning. After all, it would be little use going to great lengths to design the most amazingly beautiful coat only to discover that, a) we couldn't afford to make it, and b) we didn't have the skill needed anyway! This may sound obvious, but the garment you design must be, on all counts, the one you want to, can and will make - even if you don't personally intend to wear it. So let us take a look at these angles to see what motivates some designers, and maybe at the same time we will be able to see where *we* fit in.

The yarns: these are so exciting to some people that they are almost the over-riding reason why they knit or crochet at all. To handle the different yarns, trying to mix them and find ways of making use of the best ones without the whole exercise becoming too expensive is very mind-bending. Many people actually accumulate wonderful yarns which they can't bear to use! Usually the garments produced by these people reflect their interest in the yarns themselves.

The colours: the people who are most excited by colour are usually those whose schemes are innovative, courageous and unique. Some people prefer to take a hand in dyeing their own to achieve a totally one-off effect each time, and their garments are designed around the colour rather than the other way round. Alas, too many designers push the choice of colours so far back in their list of priorities that it appears to be totally arbitrary.

The simplicity: for all kinds of reasons, some designers' garments are so utterly simple and wearable that the rest of us wonder what all the fuss is about. These people have a knack of being able to produce garments based on the simplest possible lines with just enough difference from the norm to make them look fabulous. They may be full-length coats instead of jumpers, long caftans or tiny beaded boleros - whatever they are you wonder why *you* couldn't have thought of something as stunningly simple, and if you have already, why doesn't it look like that? More investigation needed here!

The pattern: knowing that this has to be written and produced for 'general consumption' is something which must be taken into account by designers from time to time, thus somewhat cramping their style. When you have to consider that whatever one designs must be translated and understood by other knitters or crocheters, you are then prevented from popping in an extra bobble here and there, or introducing more yarns just for extra effect. Consequently, designers in this category usually have to aim for simplicity of duplication.

Skill (or lack of it): how many times have we all desperately wanted to make something we have seen and then realised that our skills were insufficient? Let's face it, some designers are more technically skilled than others, and those who are see no reason, (quite rightly), why they shouldn't make it obvious. So their designs are produced for the opposite reasons to those who design for simplicity, (not that the 'simple' designers may not be skilled, you understand), and show the most amazingly complicated tucks, ruffs, pleats, basques, puffs, slashes, bits and bobs which intimidate and delight the rest of us. When the technical skill matches the colour-sense and the imagination, that's fine, but these don't necessarily go hand in hand.

The imagination: when all is said and done, this is the elusive element so vital to all designers, in whatever medium. At this point I'd like to send a special message to those who fear that their imagination has been left to go rusty; take heart. There are various ways of feeding it, stimulating it and generally getting it back into working order, and some suggestions are dotted about throughout this book.

One important trigger is to look very hard and carefully at other people's garments, knitted, crocheted and otherwise, resisting the temptation to dismiss them as not something you'd like to wear. Instead, try to assess their interesting features, such as cut, structure, shape, colour, pattern, yarn, texture, size, complexity or simplicity. Make mental or written notes on whatever catches your interest to see how techniques have been exploited and mixed together; look out for clever details and observe how colours and patterns have been used. Try to assess your own work *in comparison* with what you have seen and ask yourself if there is any way in which you can change for the better.

Don't ever be so deeply involved with the business of garment-making/designing that you miss out on the feed-back you need to keep your imagination alive and healthy. This means that you must be aware of visible things and absorb what you see to build up a kind of mental reference library of ideas. Our failure to notice things around us, colours, textures and patterns is reflected in our work, and our designs then become ordinary, run-of-the-mill and even dull.

Where do we look? The following lists may help. And when we've looked? Make notes, mental, written and graphic, and remember what you see. Photograph things instead of people, and keep them filed for easy reference. Be organised about this; the 'design' is the part that *shows*; it is the bit that reflects the way you are and think; it is statement of your personality. It affects people who see it as well as the ones who wear it; it affects their feelings and responses. After all that effort, do you want your garments to look so ordinary that no-one takes a second glance?

The following suggestions are just a few of the ways in which you can feed your imagination.

Ideas for pattern

All aspects of nature, skin, fur, leaves, feathers.
Stone, brickwork and architectural details.
Rugs, carpets, all types of weaving.
Mosaics and tiles, ancient and modern.
Graphs, abstract, lettering, geometric.
Flowers and plants, landscapes and aerial views.
Textiles – look in museums and glossy magazines.
Accidental patterns, marbling, soap bubbles, raindrops.

Ideas for texture

Pebbles and rocks, strata and minerals.
Lichen, fungi, mosses and grasses.
Nature's textures - bark, clouds, volcanoes, wood.
The plant world, especially fruit and vegetables.
Underwater, coral, seaweed, marine life.
All textiles; all types of constructions including lace, knitting, crochet, weaving and embroidery.

Ideas for colour

Paint shade cards.
Advertisements, catalogues, especially fabric.
Photos, paintings, magazine cuttings, postcards and books.
Stained glass and ceramics. Look in shops.
Flowers, gardens and plants.
Butterflies and other coloured creatures.
Yarns, multi-coloured, random-dyed.
Textiles, oriental rugs, visit exhibitions.
Learn the basics of colour-theory; you will be surprised at the new light this will shed on some of the things you have been doing, (right or wrong), with colour.

The unshaped garment

Far from being a way of 'opting out' of the problems attached to garment shaping and structure, the unshaped garment is as old as time. It still abounds in every country of the world where people make and wear clothes, being the most economical of effort and materials. The old English smock is a perfect example of this, being traditionally made from one length of cloth with no wastage whatsoever, and in a splendid book published by The Royal Ontario Museum, Toronto, called 'Cut My Cote' by Dorothy Burnham, a whole range of garments is presented which are made with the same end in view.

To designers, the advantage of this method is that any shaping is kept to a minimum, the accent being on aspects of colour-patterns, gathers, fastenings and other more complex details. I'm all for this! Anyway, I actually *like* the way that straight pieces drape, fold and hang. I like the way that one's bulges are gently passed over, and the loose warmth of a wrap-around hand made fabric over a cool shirt. And I also like the rather 'ethnic' feeling that goes with it!

Necklines

Although the diagrams give the impression that without careful shaping, all are square, I have found that by casting off to make the neck opening, and then by casting on again at the other side, the neckline assumes a rounded shape as soon as the edge is neatened. This can be done in one of two ways;
a) by picking up stitches in the usual way and knitting up a shallow neckband.
b) by crocheting a narrow border around the edge perhaps to complement the front and sleeve edges.

Where the front and back body pieces are left straight across at the top to form a slashed neckline and a neckband of some kind is required, first make two small triangular pieces and set one of these into each of the shoulder seams. Leave the stitches on a length of yarn while the two pieces are sewn in, then incorporate them into the neckband stitches as you pick up *but do this in two halves*, back and front separately so that they can be worked on a straight needle; otherwise use a shortish circular needle or a set of four.

If, however, you are working in crochet, this is not a problem, as rounds can be made as easily as rows.

ties of crochet chains, finger cords or French knitting

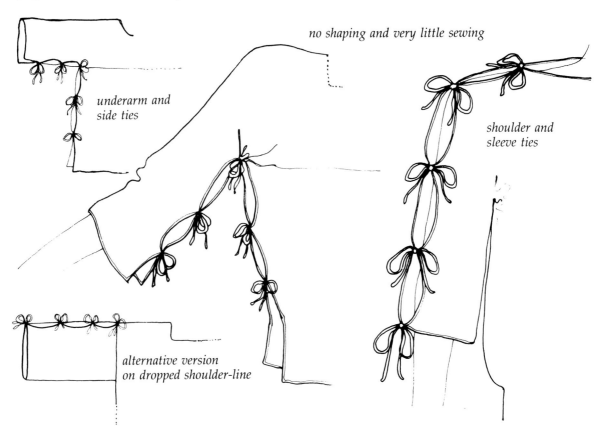

no shaping and very little sewing

underarm and side ties

shoulder and sleeve ties

alternative version on dropped shoulder-line

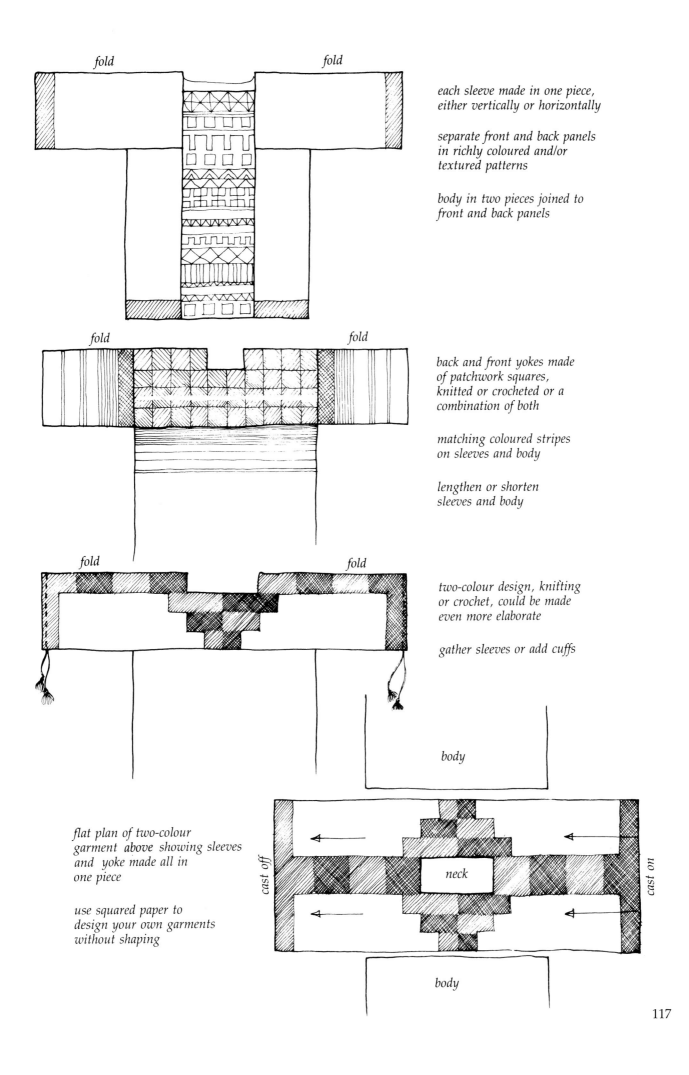

fold   *fold*

each sleeve made in one piece, either vertically or horizontally

separate front and back panels in richly coloured and/or textured patterns

body in two pieces joined to front and back panels

fold   *fold*

back and front yokes made of patchwork squares, knitted or crocheted or a combination of both

matching coloured stripes on sleeves and body

lengthen or shorten sleeves and body

fold   *fold*

two-colour design, knitting or crochet, could be made even more elaborate

gather sleeves or add cuffs

body

flat plan of two-colour garment *above* showing sleeves and yoke made all in one piece

use squared paper to design your own garments without shaping

cast off   neck   cast on

body

Fastenings

In keeping with the simple style of the 'no-shaping' garment, it is my general feeling that the fastenings which look best are the old-fashioned ones, such as ties, buttons and toggles. Dorset buttons, (see page 90), look particularly well with these styles as they were actually used on these simple garments many years ago, and now similar foundations can be bought which resemble them exactly. Ties can be made of finger cords, crochet chains, French knitting or knitted cord, and these can be used to good effect in a decorative way, (see page 116), where they can take the place of the more usual fastenings. Bare brown arms, or matching sweater or shirt look equally well under these features, and a metallic thread incorporated into the ties will add extra interest.

Avoid making the ties too heavy or thick; some brushed, furry yarns do not give crisp results, so consider using a smoother yarn of the same, or contrasting colour instead. The ties can be threaded through small spaces left between the garment and the edging.

Gussets and insets

Small triangles and squares used as insets to allow more room for movement are an intrinsic element in this type of garment, serving both functions of comfort and economy. Though not vital to comfort in every case, they are useful features which allow the addition of neckbands as in some traditional Guernsey-type jumpers. They are often decorative too, as they can be made in contrasting patterns and/or colours.

The illustrations below show how a square can be set into the underarm seam to give extra room, and in the top version, an acute triangle is set in. These shapes are easy to make separately, though care must be taken to make both sides exactly alike. Write your instructions down and measure accurately the positions on the body and sleeves.

The two small diagrams, top left, show how back and front insets can complement the sleeve decoration while at the same time simplifying the shape of the sleeve. The pieces needed for this jacket would therefore be all rectangles, as follows:

a) front/back body, all-in-one.
b) two sleeve rectangles with cable along centres.
c) two small cabled panels for front.
d) larger cabled panel for back.
e) cable pockets (not shown).

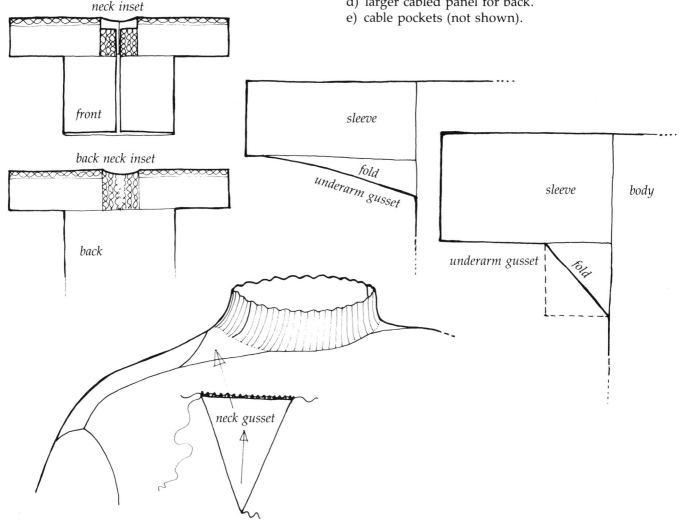

Long strip coats

These two coats are a most valuable addition to any wardrobe, being easy to make, elegant and comfortable to wear, they are made of long narrow strips of knitting sewn together, (see pages 122 and 123). The idea is not new, (nothing ever is, is it?) but I adapted it to suit my own requirements, as I hope you will.

Whenever I travel by train I like to have some knitting and crochet to do, yet long needles and rows and large bundles of fabric are difficult to manipulate. Long, narrow lengths seemed to be just the answer. These two coats were mostly made on train journeys over two years; an easy pick-up and put-down exercise yet not mechanical enough to be tedious.

Materials

Over several months I collected together any 3-ply Shetland yarns I could find, until I had between 12 and 13ozs/300 and 400gms of all colours. One coat is based on a neutral background and the other on a grey background, so quite a large proportion of the base colour was required. I needed only about ¾oz/25gms of each of the other colours and when I ran out of one yarn I simply used another. Nothing needs to be exact, and if the colours chosen are carefully co-ordinated the effect will be good.

The yarns were knitted in stocking stitch on size No12/2¾mm needles, but any other stitch pattern can be used as long as you remember that *some* patterns, such as cables, tend to draw the fabric in to make it narrower.

Length

Decide how long you want your coat to be; take a tape measure from the front hemline over one shoulder to the back hemline and make a note of this length. Each of the strips should be made to this length, but because it is difficult to measure accurately while the knitting is on the needle, it is safest to count the rows based on the tension you obtain.

Strips

The narrow ones are 20 sts wide; 2½ full lengths are needed. The wide ones are 48 sts wide; 2 full lengths are needed, (see diagram right).

To make a coat with a wider body, as seen on the one with the front fastening, two more narrow strips were inserted from one cuff along the underside of the sleeve, (i.e. between the two side edges) and down each side to the hem. This is not shown on the diagram. This should be done after the main pieces have been assembled, with the exception of the underarm and side seams, so that an accurate measurement can be made. Each strip has a crochet edging worked along each side and it is these edges which are sewn together.

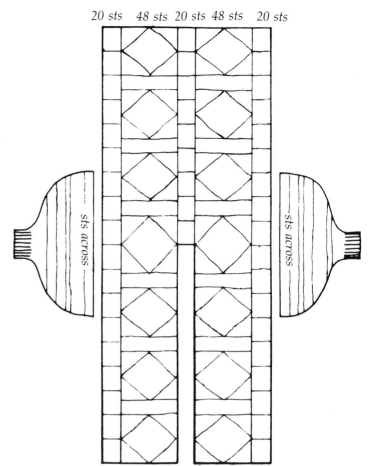

20 sts   48 sts   20 sts   48 sts   20 sts

sts across

sts across

layout of coat without crochet insertions not strictly to scale

Back view of the coat with a grey background.

119

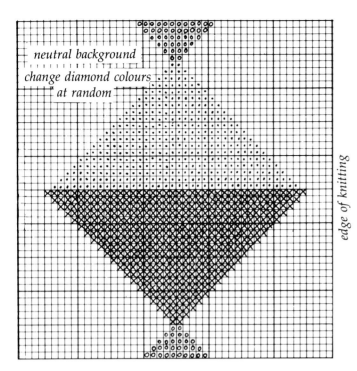

neutral background
change diamond colours
at random

edge of knitting

some simple two-colour patterns for use between the diamonds

Patterns

A basic pattern of large diamond shapes has been used on the examples shown on these pages, and, on the grey one, (see page 122), in-between rows of smaller patterns have been worked. While keeping to this general arrangement, you can use a random arrangement of patterns of all kinds.

The two sides are not exactly alike, but they balance in colour and design. For the narrow strips, checked effects look good, and note that plain blocks of colour are equally effective when separated by the base colour. If many different coloured yarns are used along the same row, instead of keeping them on the ball, wind small amounts on to card bobbins or just break off sufficient lengths. Tie on another length whenever more is needed, and keep on knitting right through the knot with the double yarn, so that no ends are left hanging on the wrong side. The extra thickness of yarn for so few stitches will not make any difference to the fabric. This is the way to avoid balls of wool getting tangled while knitting in several colours. Don't forget that to avoid a gap in the fabric, the two yarns must be twisted together at the back of the knitting where different colours meet along the row.

Making up

When all the strips have been completed, they must be blocked out and pressed, and this is something you *can't* do on a train journey! Take time to do this carefully, without stretching the fabric. To neaten the edges use a size No 11/3mm crochet hook and the base colour yarn and work 2 rows of half-trebles into both side edges of every strip. Bear in mind that crochet tension is different from knitted tension and that crochet stitches are fatter. You may have to experiment a little at first to avoid getting the edges too tight or too slack.

As a general guide, it will take 2 crochet stitches to every 3 rows of knitting. These 2 rows of crochet will add 1in/2.5cms to the width of each strip, making a total of about 9ins/23cms overall. If you decide not to work the crochet edges, remember to take this reduction in width into consideration.

When all edges have been added, pin the strips right sides together, and join them with the same colour yarn using a blunt needle. To avoid bulky seams use an over-and-over stitch, taking in the extreme edges of every crochet stitch. Insert the half-length narrow strip into the back section, and work one or two more rows of half-trebles up the two front edges and across the back neck.

Sleeves

These are made both the same, in complete pieces in the conventional way. They are very wide at the top end, resulting in a dropped shoulder line, and the underarm sleeve seam is 16½ins/42cms. Begin at the widest part nearest the body and include any pattern of your choice.

Back view of coat with neutral background.

Cast on 160 sts and work in stocking stitch, or own choice.

Work 9 rows.

10th row (dec row) (k8, k2 tog) 16 times, to make 144 sts.

Work 9 rows.

20th row (dec row) (k6, k2 tog) 18 times, to make 126 sts.

Work 9 rows.

30th row (dec row) (k4, k2 tog) 20 times to make 106 sts.

Work 9 rows.

40th row (dec row) k2 tog across all sts to make 53 sts. Work one more row.

Using base colour, change to double rib for the cuff and work as many rows as required, about 25–30. Cast off.

Press the sleeve gently into shape. With RS together, pin the cast on edge of the sleeve to the side edge of the coat, matching the centres exactly, and join as before. Now with the RS together, pin the underarm sleeve seam and the side edges together, and join.

Edges

The front edges of the grey coat do not fasten but it has several rows of half-trebles worked all the way round the lower and front edges.

The neutral coat, with the extra under-arm panel, has a welt of about 10 rows of knitted double-rib picked up from the lower edge. Use a circular needle long enough to pick up all the sts and work in rows without joining the stitches into rounds. Crochet the front bands and back neck, incorporating button holes about every 4ins/10cms along the right hand edge.

Using the same yarns, the buttons are made on plastic bases which can be bought at haberdashery counters for this purpose. This gives a unifying touch to the garment.

Aftercare

Even before being photographed, these two garments have been washed many times, so there is no cause for concern. Wash gently in *warm water* and a liquid detergent especially recommended for woollens, but *do not agitate* as this causes shrinkage.

Handle gently, rinse thoroughly and press to remove excess water. Do this several times until water is clear, then fold carefully and place in a spin-dryer for only about 2 minutes on the slowest programme. To dry, lie the coat out flat on towels placed on a table or the lawn, in the shade, and ease carefully into shape. While drying, turn over once or twice, easing the shape, and when *almost dry* finish off in a cool tumble-dryer.

Never hang your coat on a coat-hanger, but fold away in a drawer or cupboard. You may need to press the coat gently after washing, but this is by no means inevitable.

Notes on tension and measurements

Using 3-ply Shetland wool on size No 12/2¾mm needles, the tension should be 15 sts and 20 rows to 2ins/5cms.

Each wide panel will measure 6ins/16cms across *before* the addition of the crochet edges.

Each narrow panel will measure 3ins/7.5cms across *before* the addition of the crochet edges. For extra panel width, read on.

Overleaf
The two versions of the long coats shown on pages 122 and 123 are made in strips and then sewn together. They perfectly illustrate the use of colour set against a neutral background of either grey or natural. Left: the coat with the grey background and no fastening can be seen on page 119. Right: the coat with the neutral background and buttons can be seen above.

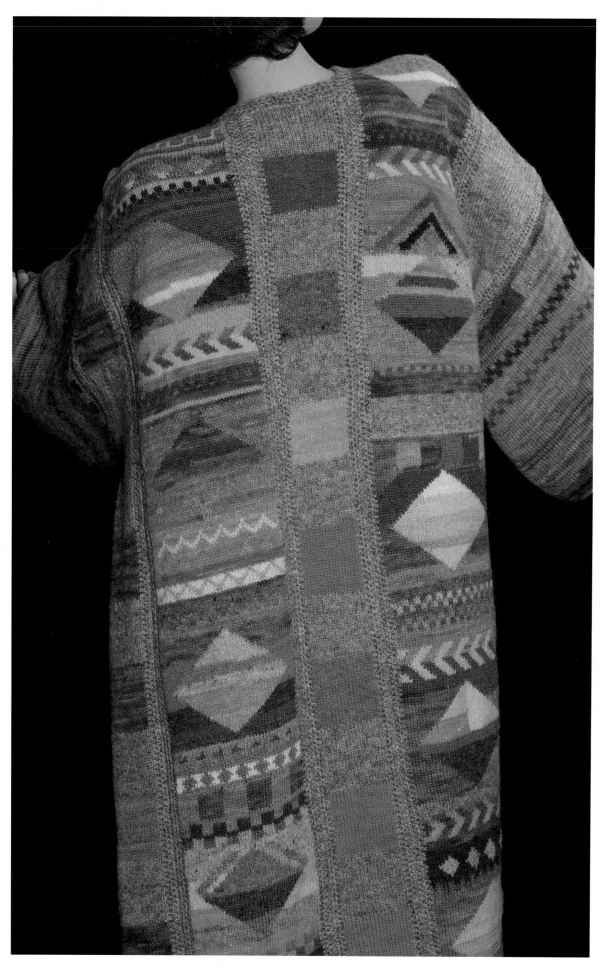

Inserting an underarm panel·

The diagram on page 119 shows how the long narrow strips of knitting are arrranged; two wide strips enclosed by two-and-a-half narrow ones; the half is the centre back panel.

As there is no armhole shaping, the dropped shoulder-line comes well down on to the upper arm and the sleeves are therefore measured from this point to the wrist. They can be as wide as you wish and stitches can be picked up from the edge of the coat and knitted on, or the sleeves can be made separately in the usual way, from the wrist edge, then sewn on to the body piece.

The crochet edges to each strip of knitting can clearly be seen in the two photographs, and on the neutral/pastel coat, the extra narrow panel can be seen on the right of the picture continuing up the side, and along the underside of the sleeve to the wristband. This extra panel is *not* shown on the diagram but can easily be inserted if extra width is required. Each of these panels measure 4ins/10cms wide, and to find out the required length, first sew up the other panels and attach the sleeves without sewing up the underarm seams. Laid out flat, with the sleeves attached, measure from the wrist ribbing to the hem of the coat and make the two long strips of knitting to the same length. Begin to sew this in place *before* casting off and you will then be able to adjust the length more exactly, but be sure to work the same number of rows on each side.

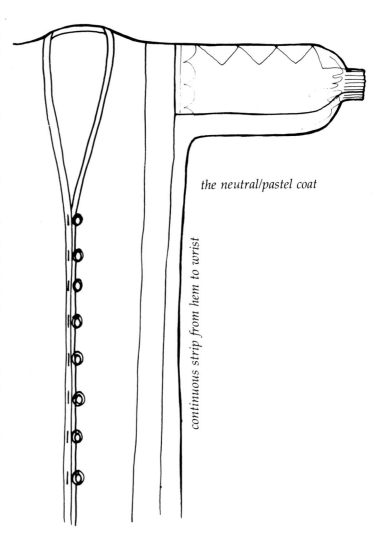

the neutral/pastel coat

continuous strip from hem to wrist

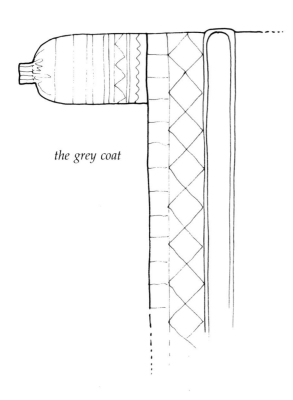

the grey coat

124

Designing with stencils

This is one of the most rewarding and exciting ways I know of making instant designs on garments. This method does not produce the shape and structure of the garment, and this is something which must be decided at the beginning when the stencil is made.

The diagram, below, shows two garment shapes, with a possible third being an elongation of the straight jumper. One of these is of the 'no-shaping' variety; the other is a batwing sleeved sweater, these two being ideal shapes for this exercise. Copy these diagrams singly on to thick paper or card, leaving plenty of space around the edges. Cut out the shapes carefully, leaving a hole where the jumper was; this is now the stencil to put over any one of a variety of suitable backgrounds.

Backgrounds for designs

These can include such examples as magazine cuttings; postcards and photographs; aerial views; abstract paintings; newspaper headlines and lettering of all kinds; patterns on fabrics; garden pictures; pieces of patterned knitting or crochet; children's drawings and paintings; your own paint/coloured pencil/pastel sketches - in other words, anything you find which will amply fit the stencil shape. Try placing the stencil in all directions.

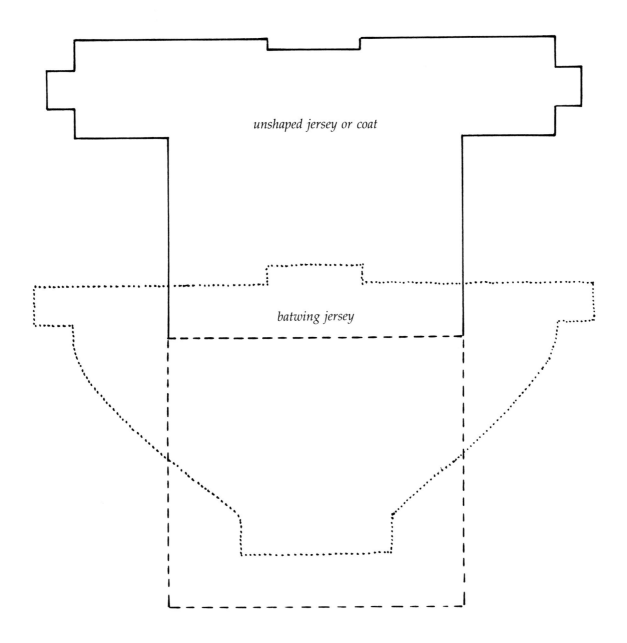

unshaped jersey or coat

batwing jersey

These illustrations show how the stencil has been placed over an advertisement at two angles, giving completely different results. You are sure to find many delightful and astonishing designs in this way, often in unusual colour combinations.◁

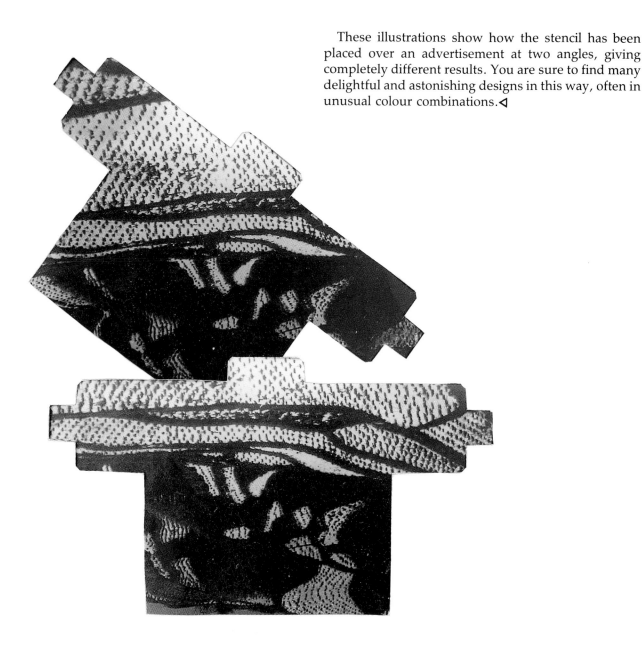

Methods of design

Having found several superb ideas in this way, here are several methods of proceeding.

a) Choose colours. Decide how many you might need; make a list, taking into consideration the different tones you may also require. You might also need to make a list of symbols for each colour.

b) Decide on the type of yarn. Make a tension swatch using the yarn you have in mind; this will tell you how many stitches you need, the correct needle size and the number of rows to the in/cm. This stage is important.

c) Estimate how much yarn. This is tricky, as it will be virtually impossible, at this stage, to say how much of which colour you might need, but one method I

use, (the other being sheer guess-work), is to weigh a garment similar in size and yarn-type on the kitchen scales. Then I try to estimate the *proportions of the colours* needed against the total weight, and always allow for some extra. Always keep the ballband so that you know what you have used.

d) Being courageous and reasonably competent, you may wish to work the design 'by eye', just as the 'Scottish Islands' panel was made, see page 37. This is a perfectly feasible way and is no more risky than remembering a basic recipe in cooking, being much easier to execute than would appear. After all, 'mistakes' are not going to be too easy to spot, are they?

e) You may prefer to chart the design, especially if it is a fairly precise one, (see page 120). For this method, enlarge the design by free-hand to the actual size required and use *tracing graph paper*, obtainable from art and good office supply shops, to trace off the shapes, using the symbols already devised for the different colours. Each square will represent one stitch, but don't forget one important point; whereas graph paper shows *squares*, knitted stitches are *not square*. Some distortion is therefore bound to occur unless you can find the type of graph paper made especially for this purpose in exactly the right guage, and for this, you will need that tension swatch! It pays dividends to do a little experimenting at this first.

The illustrations show how narrow strips of card can be wrapped with coloured yarns and laid side by side to form a rectangle.

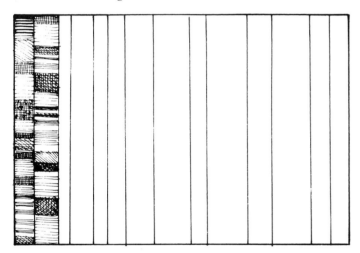

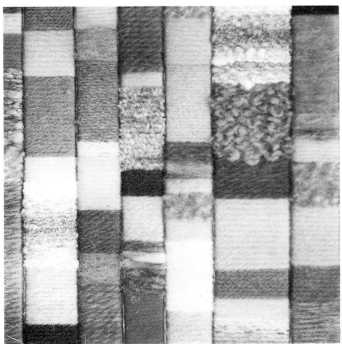

These illustrations show how the stencils have been laid over this rectangle of wrapped strips to produce a patchwork effect. They can, of course, be laid at different angles and not just in the centre of the rectangle.

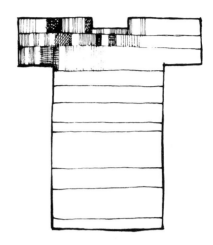

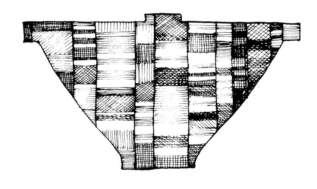

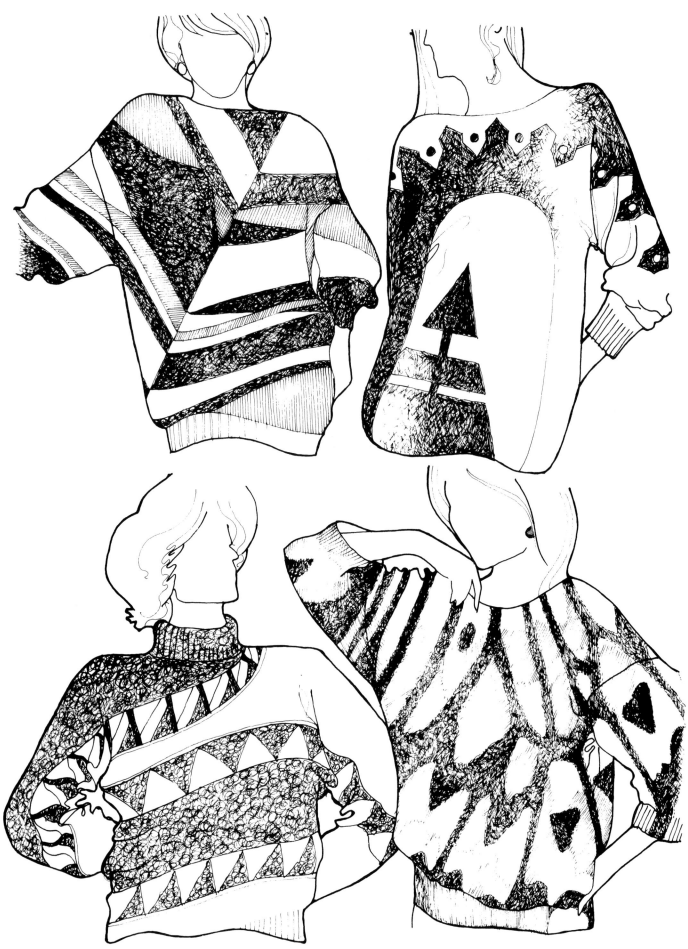

Some suggestions for jersey designs made by using stencils

Using samples

As we have seen in the previous chapters, almost any idea which can be used on a wall hanging can also be used on a garment, whether made in flat stocking stitch colour knitting, or the highly textured free-style method of combined techniques. Indeed there are many times when one may set out to 'doodle' with an idea, thinking that it may eventually be used for a cushion cover, only to see it develop in such an exciting way that, before you know it, you're wearing it! This has happened to me on more than one occasion, and I'm sure it may happen to you once you've been bitten by the designing bug.

The designer, whose work is shown below, often tries out her colours on small samples before launching into a full-scale garment. This helps to establish how the colours will react together when knitted, because,

as previously mentioned, they *do* behave differently when seen in balls or hanks and when knitted up. Tones you may have thought quite different will disappear without trace in some lights, and contrasts may clash too much!

For this three-quarter length jacket, three strands of 2-ply yarn were used together, changing one strand at a time to achieve the subtle movement of colour and tone featured throughout her design. Very little shaping disturbs the placing of the colours; a dropped shoulder-line accommodates the straight edge of the side seams, and the sleeves fall straight to a wide opening bordered by a folded hem. The quiet basket-weave pattern on the sleeves is softly echoed on the very lowest edge of the coat, down the front borders and round the mandarin collar.

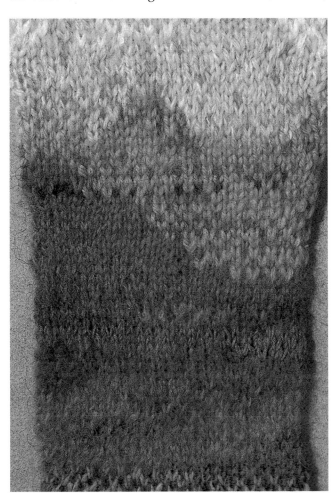

*Sample and jacket designed and knitted by **Margaret Williams***

Coat hanger designs

After all the planning, preparation, skill and sheer effort, not to mention the enjoyment, which goes into the creation of large garment, it always seems to me rather sad that they are only seen when being worn. Certainly they come alive when figures move inside them to provide the extra dimension, but many could certainly take their places alongside non-wearable wall hangings.

The answer is, of course, to originate pieces which fulfil both roles, so, meet the 'Coat hanger' designs! Nothing new, naturally, as this has been happening for many years already, but not nearly enough. Even small waistcoats make very beautiful splashes of colour and texture on a plain wall, and readers will no doubt have been excited and impressed by the colourful displays of garments in shops. So why not emulate the idea and *show* folks what we can do instead of waiting for the right moment to wear and display our talents?

An important feature of this type of project is to construct the garment, however large or small, so that it lies reasonably flat on a support. Shoulders may have to open out; kimonos and capes can hang to show either back or front.

some suggestions for coat hanger designs

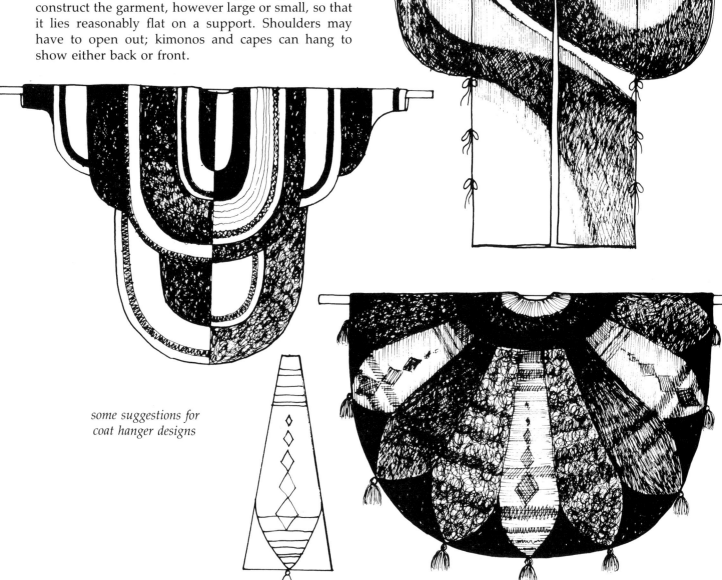

*Harmonie Brune designed and crocheted by **Kathleen Basford***

This crochet waistcoat-cum-wall hanging is based on Monet's painting of Rouen Cathedral seen in the evening light.

Measurements: 40ins/102cms long; 46ins/117cms across the lower edge.

Yarns: random-dyed chunky weight and mohair; DK mohair and bouclé, also smooth DK for some details.

The completed crochet fabric is backed on to a firm black interfacing which helps to keep it in shape.

A 'wall hanging-wearable' is a perfect illustration of the way in which a subject can be adapted to become both a garment and a wall hanging. Along the inside, (reverse side), edges of the back panel are five crochet 'buttons' which, when the transformation to garment

Landscape coat designed and crocheted by **James Walters**

is required, are attached to five of the loops along the fronts. These loops continue along fronts and back to provide a means of hanging the waistcoat on the wall. A glass or wooden rod is ideal for this purpose.

The various sections were not sewn together but crocheted on from all sides. This is where crochet has an advantage over knitting, in that shapes can easily be added on to the fabric whatever their complexity, simply by hooking into the edges, whether at side, top or bottom.

The regular lines of buildings provide a good basis for garment design, their verticals and horizontals being easily adaptable to the shapes of long waistcoats and jackets. Try this idea out for yourself using designs based on skyscrapers, your own house, tall churches and cathedrals, bell towers, castles and grand houses with formal gardens.

If most of the lines in your design are vertical, you may find it more convenient to work from one side edge to the other instead of from bottom to top. Assess this before you begin so that you are certain of choosing the best method of construction. Some pieces may be sewn together for convenience, as long as the pieces have more or less the same density. Also, knitting and crochet can be used together but be sure that one will not outweigh the other.

The amazing crochet garment shown opposite was commissioned by Ridgeway House Farm, (a rare sheep-breeds centre), as a tribute to the ladies who hand spun the fleeces, and to illustrate the beauty of the finished product. The yarns are therefore shown in their natural, un-dyed colours ranging from pure white through tones of grey, neutral and brown and into almost black; over fifty yarns of different thicknesses and qualities.

To the creator of the coat, this posed a monumental problem, but the designer is an expert crocheter living in mid-Wales who enjoyed the challenge of such a brief. He designed and made the coat to resemble the natural colours of the border country around his home, the bare wintry ploughed fields and trees, with grey hills in the distance. The huge collar froths and billows into cloud shapes around the top, while patches of snow lie on the sleeves beyond the hedges and fences.

Continuous strips of fabric

Using continuous strips of ready-made material for knitting and crochet will produce a most unusual effect.

Both these methods of cutting fabric, (see below), will yield continuous strips. Make them about ¾in/ 2cms wide for knitting or crocheting. Corners do not matter as all irregularities will be squashed into place, but, if you prefer, corners may be snipped off as shown. Glitter, lurex and delicate fabrics, plus any others which tend to fray easily should be cut a little wider. You can knit or crochet with ribbons too, and any width can be used.

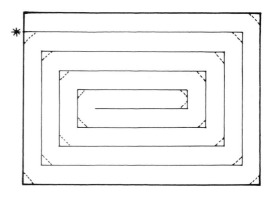

Butterfly cape designed and crocheted by **Sylvia Cosh**

Britain's leading designer of crochet garments creates fabulous designs in the most mouth-watering colour combinations for which she is renowned.

For several years she concentrated on designing and making capes and gowns based on butterfly and moth shapes, their patterns and colours being recognisable features, their flowing lines and 'wings' so easy and graceful to wear. The illustration, above, shows one of these capes worn by Sylvia herself, the graded tones varying from blue/mauve through pale plum and magenta to darker violet and navy on the wing-edges. The scalloped wing pattern is echoed on the edges of

the garment, and the back centre panel depicts the grey/black body of the butterfly. These colours and tones change frequently in each row; the stitch used throughout is a plain treble with the exception of the body for which a loop stitch was used.

The yarns, mohair, mohair-loop and chenille, were all hand-dyed by the designer, as are all her yarns for her garments, enabling her to achieve an effect of shimmering light and movement of colour-tones as the garment is worn. Like the capes shown on page 130, this 'Butterfly Cape' looks superb when placed straight against a plain wall as a wallhanging.

Free-style knitted and crocheted garments

So far, we have seen how our mixed-technique fabric can be used to produce cushions and wall hangings, but there is little doubt that its most exciting use is in the creation of garments. This poses no more problems than its use in any other area; the fabric itself is strong, elastic without losing its shape, colourful and textural, washable, warm and no heavier than any other knitted garment of the same size.

As the fabric has no particular direction, it will never pull out of shape, not even after washing. Its construction is such that it needs no pressing or finishing off, no seams to sew up either - unless you choose to make it that way. It is suitable for making into waistcoats, jackets or coats, and these may be lined or unlined.

Cutting a template

The shaping you require is achieved by using a pattern cut out of heavy duty interfacing; a non-woven variety is perfect. This fabric is cut to the shape of the garment, all in one piece and this is known as a template, (see below). When sleeves are needed, there is an extra step, but more of that later. The shoulder seams are left open so that the complete garment, minus sleeves, lies flat.

Making the fabric

Now you need to begin by making some pieces of knit and crochet fabric in the colours and yarns you have chosen. We have previously discussed the concepts behind these choices and so you will, by now, have done some trial pieces and understood how the colours move, and how the fabric is made. Remember, though, that for a wearable fabric you cannot afford too many thin patches or lacy holes, as this will not take the strain of wear and tear in the same way as denser areas, so try to keep to the same density of fabric throughout.

Let your pieces grow until you feel that they are big enough to take their place in the scheme of things, and then place them on to the template, where you think they fit and look attractive. This need not necessarily be on an edge; it may be in the middle of the back. You may even find that some of the pieces you have made fit each other rather well and can be sewn together - but don't sew them to the template! This is only to provide the shape and may be required for another occasion.

Now pin these pieces on to the template with safety pins placed from the interfacing side, as they tend to

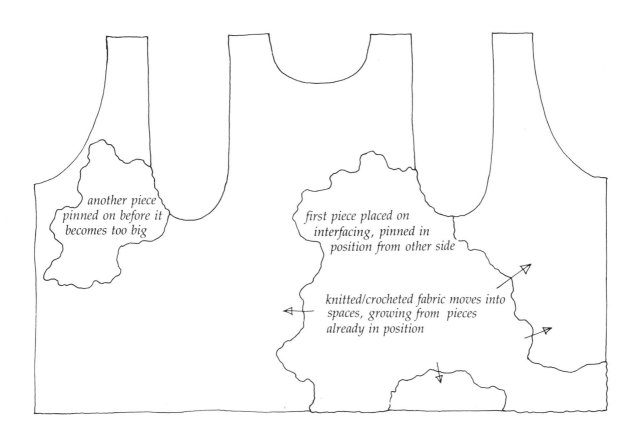

another piece pinned on before it becomes too big

first piece placed on interfacing, pinned in position from other side

knitted/crocheted fabric moves into spaces, growing from pieces already in position

135

tangle with the yarns if pinned into the knitting. Pin all the way round the edges using lots of pins, and as you continue to add to your fabric, these are undone, one or two at a time, and replaced afterwards.

When the template is completely filled, the shoulders should be either sewn in a straight line or merged into each other, depending on the shape of your fabric - the latter method avoids any bulky seams. Now you should fit the garment on to a dressmaker's form or on to yourself, to see how it looks and to decide whether you need to make any adjustments, (see below).

Welts and borders can be added if you require them but use a colour which blends with the fabric, rather than contrasts. These additions should not compete in any way with the highly-textured and colourful nature of the main fabric.

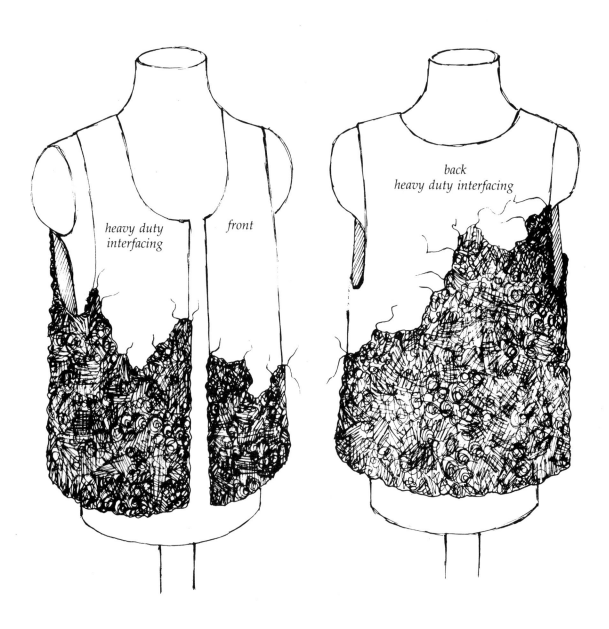

Opposite
This dramatic coat is a superb example of rich textures and subtle colours, combining all the techniques explained in this book.

Sleeves

The sleeves, if required, are made all in one with the rest of the garment, not sewn on afterwards in the usual manner. To do this, make two sleeve shapes from the same interfacing fabric and sew these on to the main template with strong tacking stitches. Try it on at this stage to check that all is well. Now the knitted and crocheted fabric is extended down the sleeve of the garment from the armhole area, (see below), working 'in the round' from the body towards the wrist end.

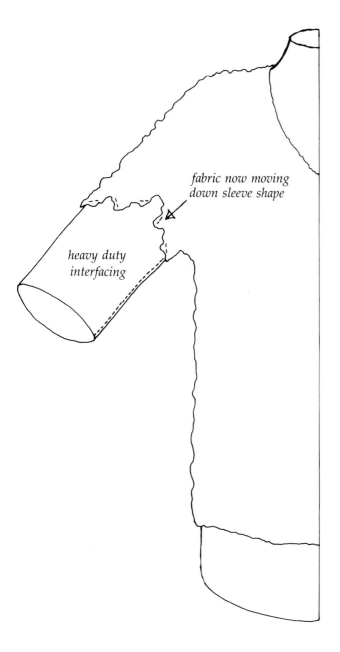

fabric now moving down sleeve shape

heavy duty interfacing

Written down in the hard light of day, (and no doubt read under the same conditions), this all sounds incredibly hit-or-miss, but really it is not as difficult as it sounds, and it works! Keep checking by putting the garment on yourself, or a model, and note the edges and dimensions. Stop whenever you want to, and try some embellishments to add colour, texture - or to cover up mistakes. Cuffs may be added if you require them, see 'Making the fabric'.

Linings

Linings are optional but do add something to the final appearance of jackets and coats where both sides may be seen. Choose a washable lining which is crease resistant if possible, and use your template as a cutting pattern.

The lining, when made up, should be hand-stitched all round the edges of the garment with a matching thread. It may also be quilted on the inside directly into the reverse side of the knitted and crocheted fabric.

Laundering

The fact that this fabric contains maybe dozens of totally different yarns of various fibres compositions and thicknesses does not pose a laundering problem. The garments which I have made in this way have always been hand washed, never dry-cleaned, and with reasonable care, nothing ever comes amiss.

Use warm water, not hot, very little, (if any), agitation, good detergent and warm or cool rinses, just as one does with pure wool. Fold, and spin on a short programme in a spin-dryer, then lay the garment flat to dry, easing it into shape. The coat seen opposite has been washed several times in this way.

Cutting the fabric

I had to take this risk, one day, when I discovered that I resembled a green pear in a waistcoat which was not long enough to cover my hips nor to sit above them! To rescue this project, I had to shorten it by at least 6ins/15cms, so I cut the offending piece off the bottom edge!

I then eased away all the tiny bits of yarn which hung precariously to the edge, leaving in place the loose stitches which would unravel if I pulled them. Then I crocheted very carefully into the edge with a matching yarn, being careful not to disturb any 'open' stitches but to deliberately hook *into* them to prevent them going anywhere. This worked perfectly; the fabric did not disintegrate, nor stretch. Now I would not go so far as to recommend this course of action, *but*, with care, one can get away with it!

Free-style decoration on plain garments

As these drawings below illustrate, there are other ways, not quite so onerous, of making use of this lovely fabric, particularly of its lace-like qualities - which one is rather prevented from doing with regard to other wearables. The irregular 'holey' effects so easily produced show to good effect when seen over a toning under-garment. This can take the form of a collar, or a decoration over a larger area spilling on to the sleeves.

A plain sweater or sleeveless pullover is a perfect foil for specially made decoration, textured or lacy, and this can be stitched on using a matching thread to become part of the garment. Glitter yarns, beads and very special threads will give new life to a jacket or jersey, and can add wonderful crunchy textures in matching, toning or contrasting colours.

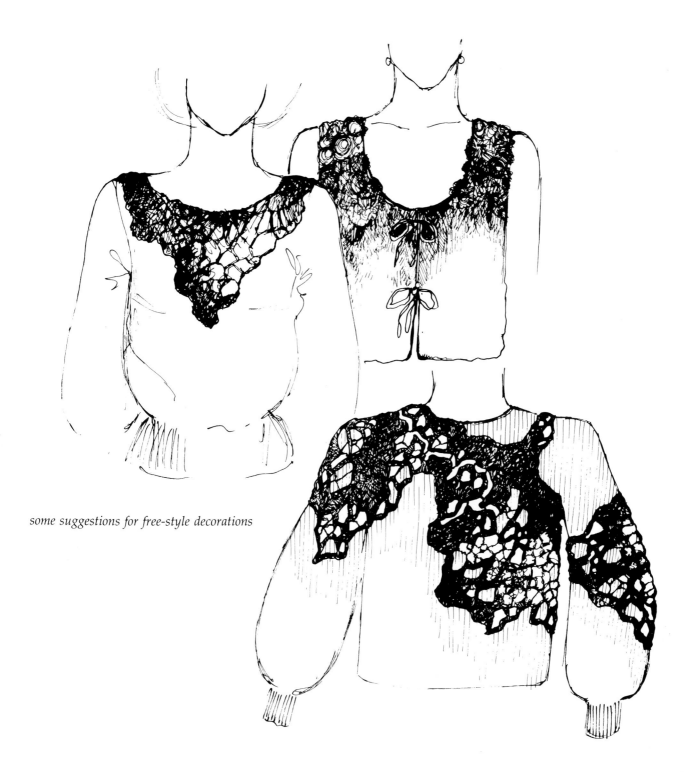

some suggestions for free-style decorations

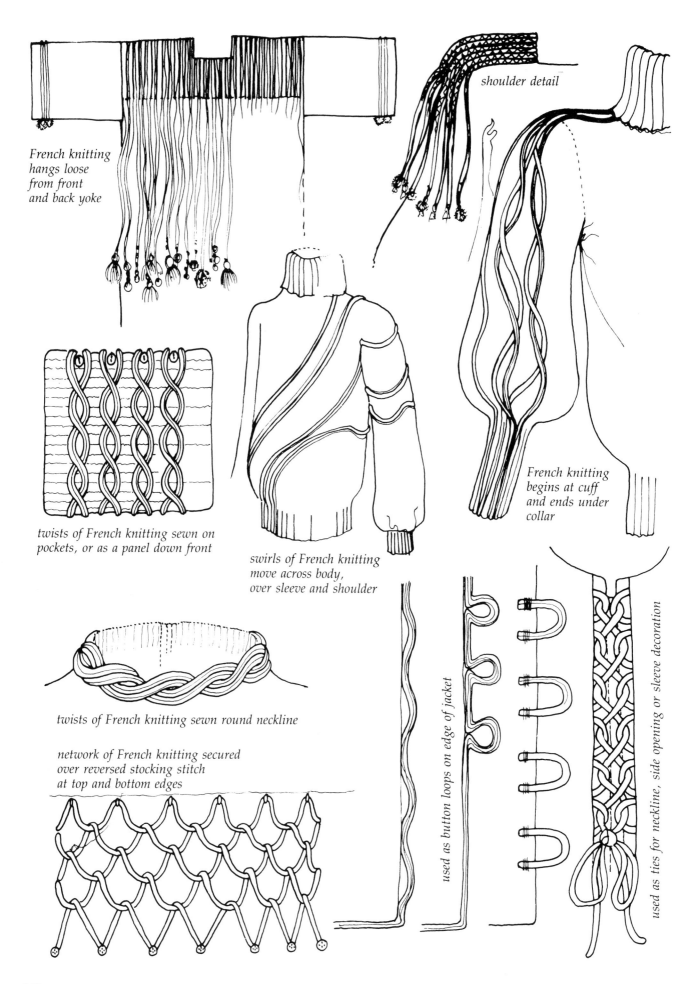

French knitting
hangs loose
from front
and back yoke

shoulder detail

twists of French knitting sewn on
pockets, or as a panel down front

swirls of French knitting
move across body,
over sleeve and shoulder

French knitting
begins at cuff
and ends under
collar

twists of French knitting sewn round neckline

network of French knitting secured
over reversed stocking stitch
at top and bottom edges

used as button loops on edge of jacket

used as ties for neckline, side opening or sleeve decoration

French knitting

This method of making a tubular knitted cord will be familiar to most readers. It is usually made on an old-fashioned wooden cotton reel, with four nails stuck into the top to act as stitch-holders. Nowadays one can buy a mechanical version which does in no time at all what used to take forever. Just turn the handle, feed in the yarn and it comes slipping out at the bottom by the yard.

To work French knitting

Though the mechanical version comes with instructions, these are brief, and do not give you all the advice you require. So here are some extra notes to save time and hassle!

First, the metal weight supplied is only heavy enough for yarns of 3 to 4-ply fineness. Anything heavier than these, such as DK yarns, need an extra weight to pull it down through the central hole. As the knitting grows, you will need to hook the weight higher up close to the machine, but keep it free; if it rests on anything it fails to be effective. The latchets will only take up to DK thickness as they are quite fine.

Threaded as shown, (see right), the tensioning device works well, but do not hold the yarn as it feeds through. Allow it to pass through the holes totally unaided, without lifting a finger, otherwise stitches may be jumped. The machine is made of plastic and may need oiling around the handle to keep it moving smoothly.

To begin

Use a large needle to thread the yarn through the tensioning device and down through the central hole then on to the weight. Allow the yarn to pass through only two alternate hooks to begin, then through the other two on the second time round.

To finish

Rest the weight on something to ease the tension. Cut the supply yarn on its free side, and pull it through the holes to the hook side. Thread the end into a wool needle and carefully slide this into each stitch on the hooks, lifting them off as you do so. Pull the stitches together and allow the end to slip through the drum and out of the bottom. Tie the ends securely to prevent unravelling.

French knitting as a trimming

Now that French knitting is easier and quicker to produce, it becomes more realistic to think about using it in greater quantities. The drawings on page 140 show some ways in which it can be used to great effect as fastenings and decorations on garments. At the top, lengths of the cord are sewn over the shoulders to hang down at the back and front, ending with tassels, bells, feathers and pom-pons. Or, from a neckline,

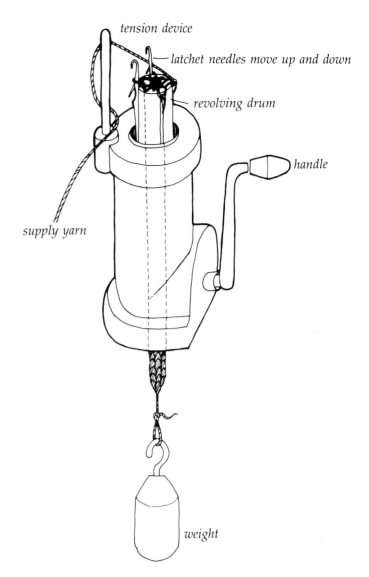

tension device

latchet needles move up and down

revolving drum

handle

supply yarn

weight

they can lie in the other direction and hang freely over the sleeve as shown.

This idea can be extended, (top right), to allow several strands to wind gently down an arm on to the cuff, or (centre), to meander across the body and sleeve back and front. Details like pockets and necklines can be given a look which belies their simplicity by sewing on lengths of different coloured cords and twisting them into a variety of patterns. Front panels of jackets, jumpers and coats can be decorated in this way. Use lengths of French knitting to create a free network of loops, (bottom left), across a yoke, or sew it along edges of jackets to make buttonholes and loops, (bottom right), like these. These can then be laced across using another coloured cord to fasten a neckline, side or sleeve seam. All my cushions are laced up in this way through a crochet-loop edge, thus avoiding putting in zips!

These are only a few suggestions; you will no doubt discover many more ideas, even plaiting, weaving and knitting it to make belts and firm fabric for bags. Experiment and have fun!

List of standard abbreviations

The following terms are standard and are used in most knitting and crochet instructions.

Knitting

dec decrease
g st garter stitch, every row knit
inc increase
k knit
p purl
psso pass slipped stitch over
rev ss reversed stocking stitch
sl st slip stitch without knitting it
st(s) stitch(es)
ss stocking stitch
tog together
yo yarn over

Crochet

ch chain
ch sp chain space
dc double crochet
d tr double treble
dec decrease
h tr half treble
inc increase
ss slip stitch
sts stitch(es)
tog together
tr treble
yoh yarn over hook
yrh yarn round hook

General

alt alternate(ly)
beg begin(ning)
cm(s) centimetre(s)
DK double knitting yarn
gm(s) gram(s)
in(s) inch(es)
LH left hand
mm millimetres
mtrs metres
No number
oz ounce(s)
patt pattern
rem remain(ing)
rep repeat
RH right hand
RS right side of fabric
WS wrong side of fabric
yds yards

Making a tension grid

The following method explains how to measure your knitting tension, and construct a grid to correspond with this, (see below).

a) Cut a window, 1¼ins/3cms square in white card.

b) In stocking stitch, knit a sample piece about 3¼ins/8cms square.

c) Pin this out on to a board and place the card window over it. Hold this firmly in place while you count the number of *stitches and rows* inside the square. Be precise.

d) Write these figures down as follows:
Tension: with DK yarn and size No.8/4mm needles measured over ss: 6 sts and 10 rows to 1¼ins/3cms.

e) Now draw another square exactly the same size as the window (1¼ins/3cms) and rule a grid which represents the tension of your knitted sample. This is now the basis of the grid on which you should chart your design to be sure of getting the proportions correct, and to avoid the distortion which happens when you use ordinary square graph paper.

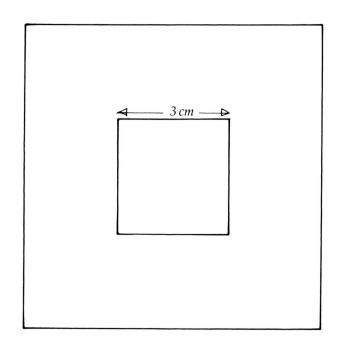

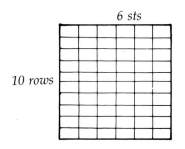

Index

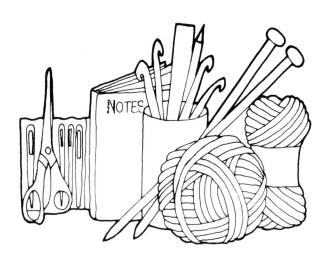

If readers have difficulty obtaining any of the materials or equipment mentioned in this book, please write for further information to the publishers.

If you are interested in any other of the art and craft titles published by Search Press please send for free colour catalogue to:
Search Press Limited, Dept B, Wellwood, North Farm Road,
Tunbridge Wells, Kent TN2 3DR